towards territorial transition

Towards Territorial Transition

PARK BOOKS

Content

I.	Introduction	10
II.	10% Fallow Matthias Armengaud	16
III.	Territorial Habitat Aglaée Degros	34
IV.	Territorial Atlas	48
V.	Territorial Portrait Anna Positano	60
VI.	Round Table Matthias Armengaud Anita Berrizbeitia Aglaée Degros Panos Mantziaras Radostina Radulova-Stahmer	88

VII. Positions 104

The making of 106
Stefan Bendiks

Valueable ecological transition? 110
Eva Schwab

Fear of the dark 113
Simon Hartmann

Who wants to start a revolution? 117
Marc Armengaud

Density and carbon emission 122
Florian Dupont

Toward a new equation 125
Matthijs Bouw

Desired density 128
Ingrid Taillandier

Territorial metabolism in digital change 131
Radostina Radulova-Stahmer

VIII. Notions 136

Scale 138
Transition 146
Territory 158
Platform 170
Resources 180
Uncertainty 190

IX. Territorial Projects — 198

Luxembourg in Transition	200
Rheinisches Revier	204
Greater Geneva	208
T.OP Noordrand	212
Raumbilder Lausitz	216
Amiter Tours	220

Appendix — 224

Biographies	225
École nationale supérieure d'architecture de Versailles student list	228
Graz University of Technology student list	229
Acknowledgements	230
Further readings	231
Bibliography	233
Image credits	236
Colophon	238

I.

Intro-
duction

This book is the result of several years of collaboration between the editors, Matthias Armengaud from AWP Paris and Aglaée Degros from Artgineering. The collaboration started in November 2020 when the international and interdisciplinary team took part in the consultation Luxembourg in Transition. The consortium was led by AWP office for territorial reconfiguration, Matthias Armengaud and Márc Armengaud, in collaboration with Matthijs Bouw, One architecture; Dirk Sijmons, TU Delft; Anita Berrizbeitia, Harvard Graduate School of Design; Aglaée Degros, Graz University of Technology; Ingrid Taillandier, ITAR and ARCADIS.

Even once the consultation, organized by Panos Mantziaras at the Braillard Architects Foundation, had come to an end the passion for the subject of territorial transition led to further involvement and ongoing exchange.

As guest professor at École nationale supérieure d'architecture de Versailles, Matthias Armengaud initiated a master design studio with Ingrid Taillandier called "Invisible Metropolis" as part of the international master's degree in "Ecological Urbanism," to which many of the consortium collaborators were invited for inputs and critiques. In a continuous process the discussion was deepened in a follow-up master design studio called "Luxembourg in Transition" supervised by Aglaée Degros together with Radostina Radulova-Stahmer at the Institute of Urbanism at Graz University of Technology.

Out of the deep exchange continuum on the territorial transition, incorporating different resources and scales, a platform emerged that integrates different networks and formats for sharing. In this sense the book is one result, but definitely not the end result, of the collaborative process moving academia and practice towards territorial transition.

Introduction

Towards
Territorial Transition

The urgency and destructive power of the climate crisis is becoming very clear as the droughts, heavy rainfall events, and floods of recent years show. Today, more and more municipalities are already declaring a climate emergency on a territorial scale. In this context, the consequences of the Anthropocene are not only making themselves felt in terms of ecology but are also having a strong economic and social impact.

Many of the "Grands Projets"—territorial projects—that have emerged in the last fifteen years focus on the spatial arrangement and management of urban and peri-urban areas, paying particular attention to quality of life by restructuring mobility, green spaces, and functions. This approach follows the idea of the city as a machine that needs to be regulated. In the course of the international calls for tenders, however, the proposals have failed to understand the city as a living organism and to use the territorial scale to understand ecosystems as essential, structuring urban units. They have also neglected to follow their eco-systemic spatial logic in the development and transformation of the city.

We have been consuming too many resources for far too long and have long exceeded our planetary boundaries. We are still dependent on global imports, which seriously affects our ecological footprint.

12

The continued dominance of private motorized transport leads to significant CO_2 pollution and sealing of ground, contributes to the consumption of fossil energy and other ressources, prevents the walkability of cities, and also raises questions of spatial and environmental justice.

We should therefore ask ourselves whether, as a whole society of humans and more-than-humans, we can afford to continue with this massive ecological extraction and excessive demand in planning.

So where do we stand today? The Sustainable Development Goals (SDGs) are a shared blueprint for a healthy planet that was established in the US in 2015. And the result of the latest SDG Report 2021 shows that—even six years after the introduction of the SDGs—there is still a great need for action in Europe. It is above all the goals of environmental protection and sustainable production that score grotesquely poorly across all countries, both in their current assessment and in their development trend.

We as architects bear responsibility for the shape of our spatial environment. But we are also responsible for the fact that more than half of the world's CO_2 emissions are caused by the building industry with its logistics, activities, and production processes—motorized mobility is certainly not the only factor affecting the environment. We therefore have the duty to use our discipline to implement innovative, sustainable design solutions.

This book addresses the enormous potential of territorial transition to enable an equitable climate- and ecology-oriented approach to systemic planning and design.

The publication starts with two essays that introduce its perspective on territorial transition. One is a plea on the topic of fallow land that discusses the necessity of territorial, eco-systemic reserves.

And the other addresses the Territorial Habitat and argues for the need for a spatialization of systems.

A photo essay provides a poetic, visual report, revealing an atmospheric climate narrative that shows an everyday life confronted with massive dangers and spatial social consequences that arise from the climate catastrophe in Luxembourg in 2021. It addresses the relation between the territory, society, and climate and makes visible the planning practices and protocols that are still strongly related to high carbon emissions and resource consumption while also revealing the consumption protocolls still inherent to our society.

An introductory round table discussion outlines the ecological transition's spectrum of meaning, addressing its relevance and necessity as well as discussing its dynamics in terms of tools, measurability, and gestalt. This discussion is complemented by eight expert contributions spanning the spectrum of topics and perspectives related to the territorial transition, revealing positions from academia and practice.

Six core notions for the territorial transition are formulated to show the different fields of action— transition, territory, scale, resource, platform, and uncertainty. Tackling these issues, student projects from two universities, L'École nationale supérieure d'architecture de Versailles and Graz University of Technology, show possible speculative spatial design approaches for a transition towards climate-neutrality.

Finally, this book spotlights six territorial, mostly cross-border projects (grands projets with a climate-oriented focus) in Europe from the last fifteen years, providing a perspective for a sustainable and livable environment: *Luxembourg in Transition*, *Greater Geneva*, Amiter, *Rheinisches Revier*, *T.OP Noordrand*, and *Raumbilder Lausitz*.

Introduction

Based on a contribution from the international and interdisciplinary competition *Luxembourg in Transition* from 2020, different systemic interactions between ecosystems, networks, uses, habitats, infrastructures, human and more-than-human spatial agents are presented in a Territorial Atlas. This superposition and visualization of the interfaces of these systems and their spatialization can make it possible to create integrated added value for all living beings on the planet on a territorial scale.

II.

10% Fallow

Matthias Armengaud

Ten percent fallowscapes is a part of an approach initiated on the "metabolism of the invisible and of the networks" carried out for ten years by AWP[1] in France to focus on the issues raised by the ecological transition and the decarbonized urban space.

Within the framework of this research, we have developed a reflection on the fallow land model. This is an alternative soil practice, a land management tool inherited from ancient agricultural techniques.

Keeping some land fallow is part of crop rotation, but it is also a particular temporality that resists evaluations in terms of productivity and immediate profit. It is therefore a strategic asset by nature, a vision for the future. However, when land is fallow this does not mean the absence of cultivation—and therefore of AWP Agence de Reconfiguration Territoriale economy—because very often this land is still planted (intentionally or not), for example, with endemic flowers. Fallow vegetation is essential, as it contributes to the reoxygenation and remineralization of the soil. The plants can also be harvested, keeping the land productive. If they were monetized in the full crop cycle, these plants would become very valuable! In terms of a strategic approach, the urban fallow can be seen as a framework for experimentation, a reserve for the next move, or a forward-looking resource. Developing urban fallow projects does not mean filling the void as soon as it has been revealed, but rather redistributing invisible qualities by setting them in motion to generate new interactions. Existing situations, currently in a state of limbo or suspense, where activities are informal, impossible, or unknown, are in fact major assets for territorial reconfiguration strategies.

[1] Founded as an architectural practice in 2003, AWP office for territorial reconfiguration www.awp.fr had begun operating in 1998 as an interdisciplinary collective running exploration workshops of postindustrial areas in Europe that would later translate into exhibitions, films, soundscapes, performances, lectures, and publications. Run by Marc Armengaud and Matthias Armengaud; once turned into a design-oriented practice, AWP started by designing a water treatment unit and several public spaces, an international research program on cities at night (the Troll Protocol),then followed numerous of architectures and large urban projects.

Planning urban fallows?

It is necessary to work the territory, not from a static position but from its different forms of existence, thresholds, and variations. This could be described as a heteronomy of the territory, articulating the slow and the fast, the ancient and the futuristic, the intense and the invisible, the existing and the possible, in specific systems, networks, arrangements, and gardens. Differentiation is the key to this approach, because the fallow state is not site-specific, but relative to a situation between sites and movements: a situation that is not active in a standardized productive way at a given moment can be considered fallow. And the fallow state is a condition for reinstating dialogue between territorial systems and landscapes.

Our recent work[2] has been undertaken in collaboration with world renowned laboratories, such as EPFL or Harvard GSD, for example, on *Greater Geneva* or *Luxembourg in Transition*,[3] projects which have allowed us to determine a proportion of 10 percent of the studied territory that could be made part of the urban fallow system. This is a negotiable and simple percentage in terms of communication, which can be used to counteract the latest climate scenarios. The observation of these territories through the network infrastructures has made it possible to highlight the existence of important underutilized land reserves multiplied by the risk factors. The example of the overhaul underway on the territory of the Achères wastewater treatment plant illustrates this intention well: in the long term, with the repatriation of the sludge treatment plant to the vicinity of the water treatment plant, the plant's footprint will be reduced to 50 percent of its current total area.

And the fallow state is a condition for reinstating dialogue between territorial systems and landscapes.

Our position is as follows: in view of the ecological problems that we must now face, these reserves must be invested in a program of urban fallow land and the creation of territorial carbon sinks.

A specific methodology?

We have paid particular attention to territorial stratification, and its relationship between time and space. Stratification is about movements and interactions, and it requires particular analysis and representation to reveal the articulation of these states: some layers are active, others are neutralized, and some are invisible, or in movement. The key to reading is perception, both as a voluntary act of observation/interpretation, as well as a physical commitment to exploring that allows the birth of a particular feeling: "territorial intimacy."[4]

2 In association with the international master of École nationale supérieure d'architecture de Versailles, the Graz University of Technology urban laboratory, the Alice laboratory of EPFL, Harvard GSD, and others.

3 See the projects in the territorial projects chapter. AWP piloted two proposals for these major consultations of metropolises in transition, which took place from 2017 to 2021. The mentioned results also follow studies and proposals on the metropolises and territories of Paris, Arles, Bâle, Frankfurt, Lyon, Athens, Helsinki.

4 Armengaud, *Le Grand Paris 2058*

10% Fallow

The smallest detail can be enough to qualify the whole (reversing the relationships of scale) and the smallest, almost invisible interventions can be enough to reweave the territory.

Our position is as follows: in view of the ecological problems that we must now face, these reserves must be invested in a program of urban fallow land and the creation of territorial carbon sinks.

Thus, setting the territory in motion is more important than the quality of its individual elements. From a perspective of sobriety and justice, it is no longer a question of proceeding by complete substitution of one model for another, but of finding new resources in what is already there.[5]

This is an analytical and strategic approach that we have called "territorial reconfiguration."

Territorial reconfiguration

Starting from reality: the sustainable conceptions of our time are inscribed in a space made of new triumphant autonomous frameworks, labels, and market shares. Nevertheless, the reality is made up of pre-existing situations that can be evaluated and incorporated[6] in their present state, and not solely taken when they become obsolete. Taking into account an examination of the network's evolution, it shows the functional reduction of the universal network through the increasing efficiency of the local loop. It results in a withdrawal of these areas from the urban continuity (privatization of macro lots, laws of exception).

[5] "The refusal to demolish modern monuments proves this, the future is no longer a destination but a reality that works for the present". Andrea Branzi, "Experimental Environment," in *diapos, abet laminate*, (1988).

[6] "These resources form a backup system in case primary water sources fail, which is a problem the city has faced before." Mars, Kohlmstedt, *The 99% Invisible City*.

Fig. 01: Climate scenarios

SCENARIO 01
Optimization strategy
+0.7°C

SCENARIO 02
Alternative strategy
+1.8°C

SCENARIO 03
Chaos management
+3.2°C

What does the future hold for the universal network?

Simplification would mean isolating incomplete archipelagos. Islands are divided up according to the reading of the site and so to different layers of which they are composed. The uncertain connections between the reading levels lead us to think in terms of peninsulas, and their translation into autonomous entities which are

defined according to their connection to the rest of the system.[7] We cannot believe in a simple situation of attachment (as in virtual network simulations) but rather in the shift of a site toward its rallying points: the commons. Who would be able to question the mutation (or disappearance) of the continuity/weave, if only to recognize the transitory conflicts: neighbors, places of production, logistics, public spaces, nature, emptiness…

We suggest that the answer lies not only in an architectural or planning discourse but in the understanding of territorial phenomena revealed by the project at several specific scales and their translation into project culture.

Which climate scenario requires which strategic attitude?

The context of the ecological transition will not be that of a linear change that follows a regular curve. Transition cannot be assumed to be a simple project of rationality substitution.

Transition cannot be assumed as a simple project of rationality substitution.

It is a paradigm shift[8]: we are moving from a linear vision of development toward the management of multiple priorities that are chaotically interrelated. There is no longer a single future to face, but several. The general evolution of climate change can be broken down into three successive phases over the 21st century.[9]

Each of them will overlap on the occasion of specific crises with potentially devastating effects: the increase in temperature will take place at a rate that remains uncertain in its progression,[10] so we propose identifying three thresholds that correspond to stages in terms of operational capacity:

+ 1.5°…. > optimization
+ 2.7°…. > alternative
+ 3.7°…. > chaos management

[7] Antoine, *La Ville Territoire Des Cyborgs*.
[8] Latour, *Facing Gaia*.
[9] Liu and Liu, *The Three-Body Problem*.
[10] IPCC, "Climate Change 2022: Impacts, Adaptation and Vulnerability."

Fig. 02: Publication about *Greater Geneva*

In other words, below an increase of 1.5 degrees, the projects that we will be able to develop (during the first fifteen or twenty years) will aim to optimize existing approaches. When it comes to the networks, it is a question of making the best of the current infrastructures, so initiating a strategic turn toward the rupture with the instruments at our disposal. These projects are available to start tomorrow, and the recent strong development of the transitional urban planning culture should contribute to this immediacy. (It is too often subject to large classic projects, yet its ability to integrate cross-cutting and innovative processes corresponds very well to the climate challenges, the design of incubators, and its link to networks.) This means the assessment of obsolescence and resilience levels, cross-border rationalization, and coordination of technical solutions, networking of networks, revaluation of rights of way, and staging of emergencies. These attitudes can have a broad spectrum of scales and applications; the issue is situating them well to involve the actors to avoid a territorial communitarization (efforts by some). Thus, the 1.5-degree stage represents a test stand for preparing and inclining the whole toward the following, almost certain, scenario.[11]

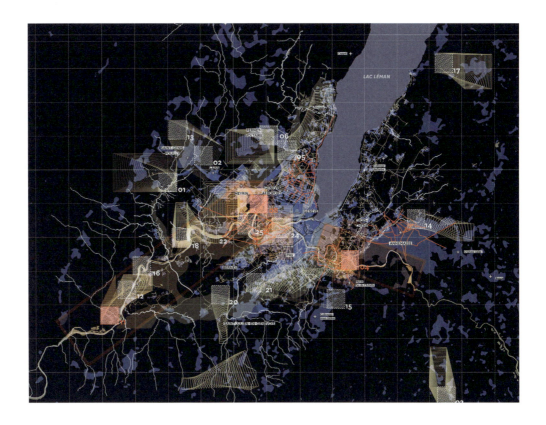

11 Rilke, *C'est le paysage longtemps.*

Fig. 03: Masterplan for *Greater Geneva*

Above 2.7 degrees, it becomes necessary to design responses differently from the present. We will be confronted with the obsolescence

of certain existing systems, even after reinforcing and increasing them, or we will be overwhelmed by the simple management of the current ones. The alternative is changing our approach to design, being able to deal with events that the current networks will no longer tolerate. For instance, stormwater basins will have to be integrally redesigned given that the urban soil and subsoil will become extremely vulnerable (floods will come from below). Nonetheless, the violence of storm precipitation could also be approached as an energy resource, for example as depolluting power. The dimension of the projects, and their interconnection, bring us away from the "urban project" to the "territory project." A perhaps more accurate translation of the Italian typo-morphological beginnings, the stage should only be pursued if it avoids the following one, or if it is confined to peaks which combined actions will gradually reduce.

Thirdly, beyond an average increase of 3.7 degrees, we enter a terra incognita: managing chaos. After this threshold, it will probably no longer be possible to pursue anything other than crisis management: accept accidents, give up solutions that require stability, or rather are too exposed to risks… In other words, the notions of territorial control will have to give rise to new, much more reactive and flexible attitudes, oriented toward collective survival objectives, the extent of which is difficult to gauge:

"Alternative": we should change the approach to design, being able to deal with events that the current networks will no longer tolerate.

the very existence of fundamental reference points, such as the seasons or the level of water reserves could be at stake…

Fig. 04: Revelation of climate scenario

22

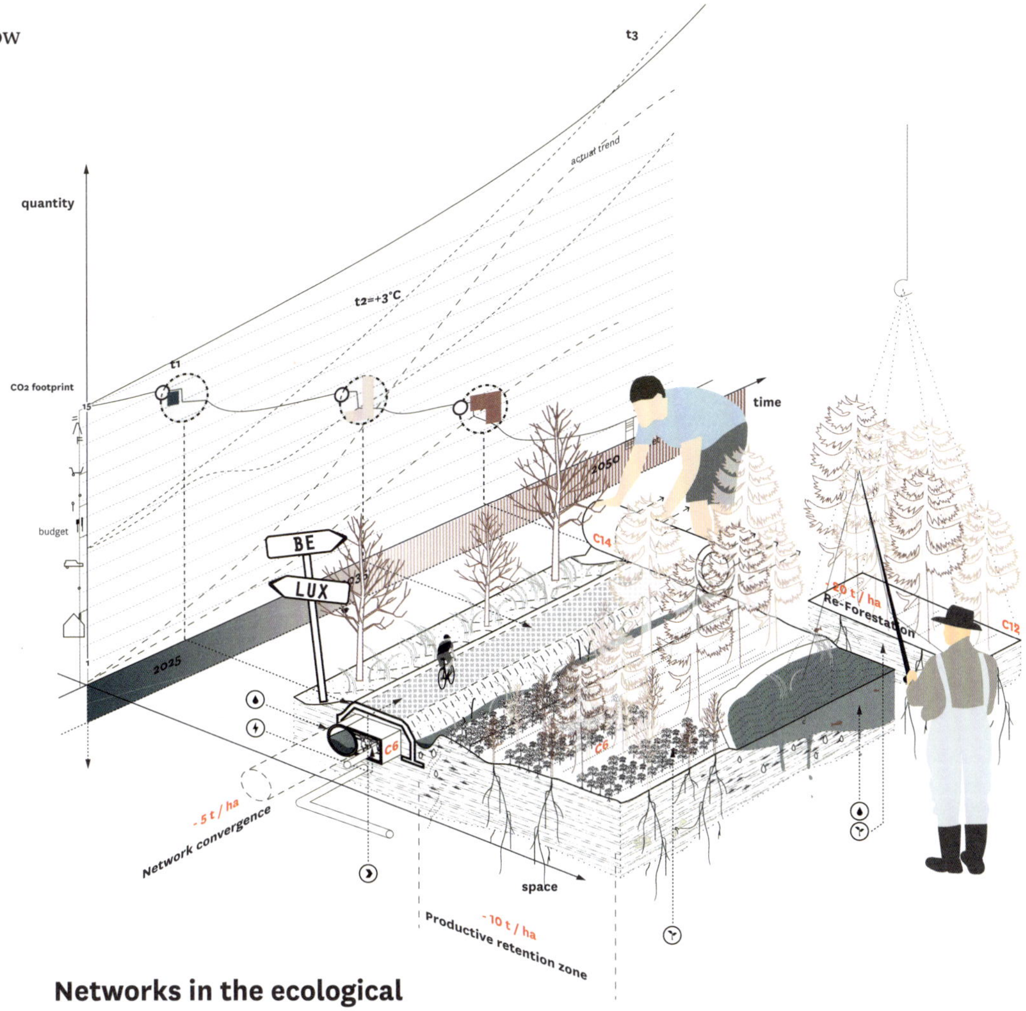

Networks in the ecological equation[12]

Networks are indicators of climate change and systemic ecological disturbances. The analysis of risks and hazards shows that networks will be subjected to successive stresses that accelerate their obsolescence in every envisaged configuration. It implies the requirement of considerable changes that must be at the heart of the ecological transition, such as the abandonment of certain networks (gas, etc.) or the multiplication of others (gray water, etc.), but not necessarily following a universal reticular network.[13] In the face of risks, it is a question of making possible mitigation and adaptation efforts, but it is also a matter of financing these efforts. In a forward-looking vision, the choices in terms of networks will play a central role in anticipating where the necessity to react will be essential. A critical analysis of the current functioning of these networks would make them converge with the objectives of the transition, and as a result figure corresponding to the forward-looking approach. Thus, it must be ensured that networks are neutral or even positive whenever possible.

12 "Network," Dictionary education. In the first place, a network designates, in a concrete sense, "a set of intertwined lines" and, in a figurative sense, "a set of relationships." By extension, it designates an interconnected whole, made of components and their inter-relations, allowing the circulation in continuous or discontinuous mode of flows. Source: Dictionary, "Network."

13 AWP led a research group on this topic with ENSA Paris Malaquais, in Paris in 2015 with urban planners and experts from Vinci, Suez-Environnement, AIA Environnement and the FING; this research was continued in the framework of the smart living lab, EPFL HESFR in 2016

Fig. 05: 10 percent urban fallow land proposal

10% Fallow

"What place for this time?"[14]
On a Thursday night, in "Grand Paris," more than three million people are working. For whom? How? Where? In which space? We consider the metropolis scale where the invisible layers can reveal, activate, and re-define the "territorio."[15]

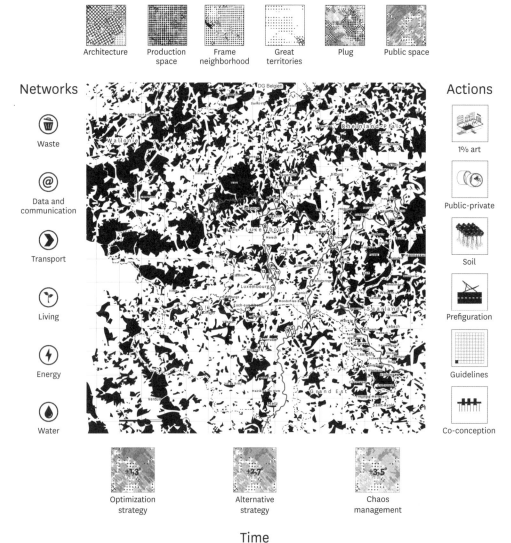

Fig. 06: Matrix of *Luxembourg in Transition*

[14] Lynch, *What time is this place?*

[15] Armengaud and Taillandier, *Invisible metropolis master studio at École nationale supérieure d'architecture de Versailles introduction text.*

[16] Moulier-Boutang and Aigrain, *Le Capitalisme Cognitif.*

[17] The negative commons can induce the idea of communities of non-use, in other words, of collectives seeking to no longer use certain entities formerly described as "resources" {...} "Remove the living from this mobilization in order to make room for unproductiveness" {...} "Heritage is first of all a continuity {...} is then a threshold {...} a charge" {...} "In the face of the organized world and its reductionisms, which reduce the world to proliferating ontologies, poor in intensity and inheriting negative commons and collapsed objects. Thus, we propose to build an ecology that gets its hands dirty. Figuratively speaking: the mechanical, mineral, metallic or chemical sludge of the Technosphere, in other words, look first to the Technosphere and deal with it." Bonnet, Landivar, and Monnin, *Héritage et fermeture.*

The invisible urban development:
The development of cities remains inseparable from the development of technical urban networks. The 19th and 20th centuries were characterized by the superposition of

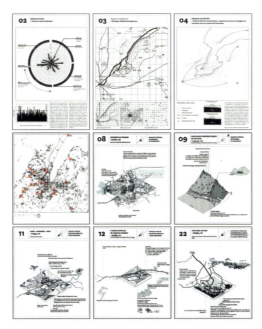

new infrastructure systems, such as drinking water supplies, rainwater and wastewater sewers, public transport, electricity, and gas distribution.

The development of cities remains inseparable from the development of technical urban networks.

The path toward equipping the urban space has led toward a condition of a higher degree of networked cities, and so toward a status of "single network": reticular in form, organized as a monopoly, and aiming at universal service.

Fig. 07: Critical atlas and site of *Greater Geneva*

Fig. 08: Networks morphology of *Greater Geneva*

Supply and service notion evolution
This "single network" model is being questioned in favor of more decentralized solutions or those based on the concept of the circular economy.[16] The central assumption is that the vital consideration of transition will accentuate these trends and reinforce a new organization based on autonomous meshes. The questioning is also

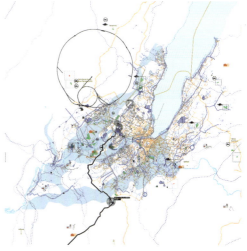

observed through transformations of the different components of technical systems:

- the rapid development of information and communication technologies;
- liberalization policies supplemented by dismantlement operations;
- the demand for an increasing individualization of community supply (mini-grids or individualized supply systems at the plot or building level, treatment of organic waste, etc.);
- the closure, or emergence, of an alter-urbanism.[17]

Incidence of networks

As the role of networks is fundamental in dimensioning the future urban grid and settlement forms, its perception will change dramatically in the future. In particular, networks will affect urban modes (living/working/producing/exchanging...), architecture, and the definition of urban metabolism.[18]

Thus, the network's strategic planning becomes a lever for sustainable and invisible strategies, and so for generating a fertile territory hidden in the folds of the visible landscape.

A discreet urbanity?

The challenge coincides with raising awareness about the networks' interface requirements in public spaces and architecture, and thus also with the possible mutations generated by their contact with each other. Meanwhile, the wider scale corresponds to the transformations created by the intersection of territory and production infrastructures.

Thus, the position of major sustainable infrastructure projects (waste, water, energy) will be crucial for identifying pivotal areas for territorial reconfiguration.

The challenge coincides with raising awareness about the networks interfaces requirements in public spaces and architecture, and so the possible mutations generated by their contact with each other.

The notion of interface refers both to the digital dimensions of the future metropolis and to the capacity of reading its variations, flexibility, and uses.

The uses determined by the future urban mesh stakeholders will redefine the perception of urban service: who are local authorities; operators, network suppliers; architects, urban

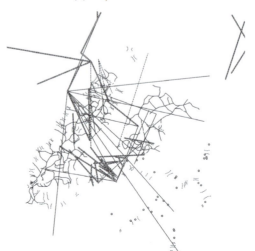

18 Sijmons, *Landscape and Energy*.

Fig. 09: Urban structure of *Greater Geneva*

Fig. 10: Networks collages of *Greater Geneva*

planners; network users; researchers; innovative companies. A tension emerges between the techno-technocratic world of structuring networks and a renewed society. A contrast between the latter that defines itself by networked practices (users are

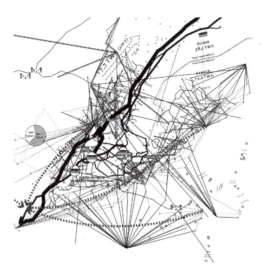

networked among each other and make use of networked networks "leapfrogging") and values and configurations (flexibility, speed, choice) which are at odds with the top-down engineering of the territory placed in a public service delegation company ("invisible" structures with gigantic budgets and capacities for action).

This provides an opportunity for designers—indeed the networks emerge in valuable territorial situations, in the hinterland and borders of cities, and in relation to great structuring landscapes (rivers, coasts, ravines, etc.), offering a unique reconfiguration and creative situation.

In a time when the metropolis has turned its back on the natural powers of its site, the necessary evolution of the technical and natural system is an opportunity to overcome the lack of room for maneuver in the face of the different territorial realities. While liberating margins, the network approach makes it possible to envisage a new systemic mesh that is reconciled with the landscape. This could involve accepting the risks of flooding or the consequences of increasing droughts, in short by integrating the natural networks

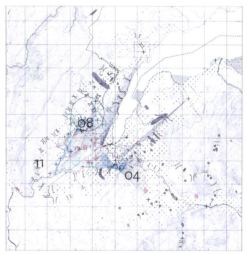

and their variations in interaction. The dialogue between networks will appear as a common denominator in most projects presented in the latter chapters.

Should public space become a resource ground? What form would it take? What would be the materiality of the network's interface? What impact would the network's

Fig. 11: Networks collages of *Greater Geneva*
Fig. 12: Identification of potential sites

innovation have on architecture? What would the landscape integration mean for the infrastructures? What would be the dimension of the network mesh? This would be a territory that emerges through adaptation and resilience. It is important to exploit the major technological potential of interconnecting networks, which are currently managed in silos when they could act in synergy (mutualization, recovery, transfer, compensation…).

Networks must now be reintegrated into their natural logic, which has been denied or underestimated (watersheds, water tables, seasonality, ecosystems, etc.), while in the long term, the final aim corresponds to the territory's ecological base rebalance through the relocation and integration of functions. These objectives are part of a desire to overcome the arising territorial contradictions. The case of Luxembourg, as described in this book, corresponds to the administrative border effect status. Indeed, a new, more flexible, and more reactive network paradigm must be applied to accelerate new cross-border cooperation—aiming at the definition of a Euro-region, or more precisely a Euro-Metropoli-torio.

The network scoreboard

Not all networks have an equal strategic value at a given moment—it depends on the territories and their situation. Nevertheless, their representation as the metabolic base for spatial planning is a common denominator, and it also represents a sophisticated political condition. Indeed, as soon as the networks weaken, the sense of community is threatened. The issue of networks is of considerable importance in the wider process that involves technical and cultural reorganization of the development modes.

Especially as the territory is over-characterized by border situations, several different conceptions of network management are encountered, according to each country's regulations. In schematizing territorial metabolisms, we can identify six families of networks and their associated territories:
- natural (geology, hydrology, ecosystems, etc.)
- water (drinking, wastewater, and runoff)

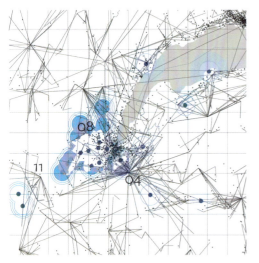

[19] Bonnefoy, *Le Nuage rouge*. Translation by editors "and this world is not so much empty as impenetrable, because ambiguity destroys all coherence, multiplies the traps, lures the eyes, as in those images that move on a roofless hovel where shadows play … In how many grizzly landscapes, like the famous Strada Bianca, is the path involved in an essential uncertainty of the values of white and black, which makes it a bump that is the void, a torrent frozen in the white night!"

[20] Laumonier, *Le Kremlin-Bicetre: Zones sensibles*. "Quand il pleut dans l'Ohio, la liquidité diminue dans le New Jersey."

[21] Fabian, Vigano, and Secchi, *Water and Asphalt*.

[22] Munarin, *Tracce di città*.

Fig. 13: Influence zone of pilot sites

28

"et ce monde est moins vide encore qu'impénétrable, car l'ambiguïté cette fois aussi détruit toute cohérence, y multiplie les pièges, leurrant d'abord les yeux, ainsi dans ces images qui bougent sur une masure sans toit où jouent les ombres…Dans combien de paysage de grizzana, comme la célèbre Strada bianca, le chemin est il impliqué dans une incertitude essentielle des valeurs du blanc et du noir, qui fait de lui une bosse qui est le vide, un torrent figé de nuit blanche!" [19]

- waste (collection, sorting, recovery, depollution)
- energy (electricity, gas, fuels, geothermal energy, etc.)
- mobility (road, rail, air, waterways, etc.)
- digital (internet, telephony, satellites, etc.)

Toward a guide plan

The typo-morphological analysis method applied to the proto-urban organs reveals new layers that should be integrated into the design strategy. This would make it possible to understand the interaction between the urban plateau and its networks: in terms of spatiality between above and below, and between inhabited spaces and autonomous lines.[20] At the same time, the analysis makes it possible to discover the areas of impact, and their link to the landscape, thus tracing lines that become networks of points, or even inhabitable ghost lines. The investigation structure is directly connected to Bernardo Secchi's methodology[21, 22]: the logic of spatial association, which illustrates the hidden meshes and uses of the ground.

Invisible for whom? Primarily for inhabitants, who hardly recognize the spatiality of common investments. Secondly, for architects, who do not integrate hidden meshes into their project perimeter, leaving them to specialists, at best ecology research offices.

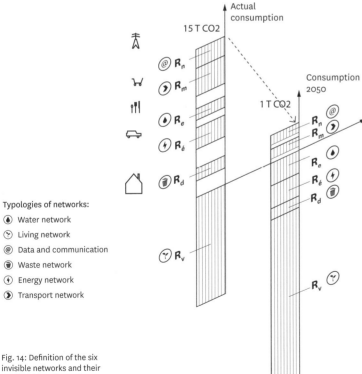

Typologies of networks:
- Water network
- Living network
- Data and communication
- Waste network
- Energy network
- Transport network

Fig. 14: Definition of the six invisible networks and their role in addressing carbon emission reduction

The changes to the network, rapid and uninterrupted, represent an obstacle to the representation and generation of habitable spaces. The challenge arises of providing the tools to bring together imaginations, budgets, and construction methods, thus creating an alternative project culture. The depart is the constitution of a homogeneous network of city centers and large planned operations, with the result of making geography disappear in favor of a universal connection. The exceptions, or aberrations, multiply as soon as we leave well-identified perimeters, approaching the hinterlands where the meshes have been dislocated. We can easily read back-to-back figures, the archipelago[23] ones on the ground and in the subsoil, despite the "islands," or the interstitial environment, appearing different. Mineralization is taking part of the liquid space: where is the soil?

As we peel back the layers, the soil shifts from simple grids to micellar figures,[24] constellations, and rhizomatic configurations.[25] These figures resemble botanical plates or atlases, usually drawn in 2D, while the challenge is a 3D reflection, as well as a four dimensional one that includes time.[26]

The first response is a classification attempt:[27] soon enough the manipulation would generate the creation of more abstract figures,[28] bringing together unknown forms,[29] lines, and features. The second stage corresponds to the elaboration of the supports integrating the temporal dimension and more varied data. The arrangement gave birth to the creation of what we call "monsters" (the monster for the strangeness, the confusion of genres, and the dazzling allowing the rebirth[30]). It represents an analysis result that tends toward the project and saturates the vision while keeping a manipulable scale.[31]

Interrogating networks means isolating frames, drawing their structure differently, and accepting their destructurization to describe an unknown alphabet.

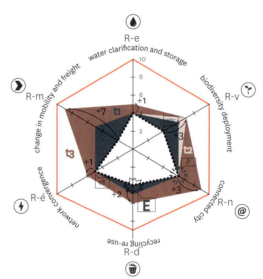

Typologies of networks	Current status	Pilot project t1	t2	t3	goals 2050
Water network (R-e)	4	4	4	5	10
Living network (R-v)	4	6	7	7	10
Data and communication (R-n)	6	6	6	9	10
Waste network (R-d)	4	5	5	6	9
Energy network (R-é)	5	5	5	6	10
Transport network (R-m)	2	5	5	9	10

23 Hertweck and Marot, *The City in the City*.

24 Ingold, *The Life of Lines*.

25 Deleuze and Guattari, *Mille plateaux*. They assert that in the rhizome "there are only lines" that intersect, influence, and delimit each other: "they transform, and can even pass into each other." In addition to the lines that could be considered structural (the molar lines and the molecular lines), other lines arise that are difficult to grasp: the vanishing lines. Those leave the framework of the structure, seek to break away, and contribute to the phenomenon of deterritorialization.

26 Bertin, *Le Graphique et le traitement graphique de l'information*. Illustrated the principle of sampling and interpolation "the point of comparison is provided by the correlation constructed on two ordered characters (…) outside the grain, the constant visibility constructs a poorly differentiated picture"; the problem of Z-bearings "making the relevant groupings readable."

27 Mangin and Panerai, *Projet urbain*.

28 Gracq: "Ce qui n'était qu'une forme, se trouvant désormais éclairé, devient le réceptacle d'un effet."

Fig. 15: Polar diagram showing network reconfiguration, current status, and spectrum of actions.

10% Fallow

Association of frames, adventures of lines

There is a frontal relationship between networks and territory.[32] The polarization derives from the linearity of the network in its main segments and the difficulty of holding and looking at them since it is constructed autonomously and often autistically to its environment.

The space can be assumed to be polarized, like banks, as with the great urban categories described by Kevin Lynch and their appliance in classifying the invisible world. Concerning ourselves, it is a complement to

29 Wikipedia, "Geographic information system." A geographic information system (GIS) is a type of database containing geographic data (that is, descriptions of phenomena for which location is relevant), combined with software tools for managing, analyzing, and visualizing those data.[1] In a broader sense, one may consider such a system to also include human users and support staff, procedures and workflows, body of knowledge of relevant concepts and methods, and institutional organizations.

30 Shepard, *Le maître de miniatures*.

31 Michaux, *Saisir*. "Qui n'a voulu saisir plus, saisir mieux, saisir autrement, et les êtres et les choses, pas avec des mots, ni avec des phonèmes, ni des onomatopées, mais avec des signes graphiques ? Qui n'a voulu un jour faire un abécédaire, un bestiaire, et même tout un vocabulaire, d'où le verbal serait exclu ?"

32 Bailly, *Le Dépaysement*.

Fig. 16: Typologies of interventions

Land art	Folie	Backfill	Production	Batofar
Art	Public funding	Network	Workshop	Drive-in
Hinterland	Icon	Stock	Green infrastructure	Compatibility
Biennal	Optimization +1	Ground naturalization	Node	Wilderness
Situative adaptation	Infrastructure	Nature invasion	Covid-19 friendly	Transhumance
Temporary	Pedagocial path	Runoff	Street food	Void
Frame the landscape	Hollow	Rave party	Playground	Optimization -1
Correspondence	Workshop	Fab lab	Frame	Make it

10% Fallow

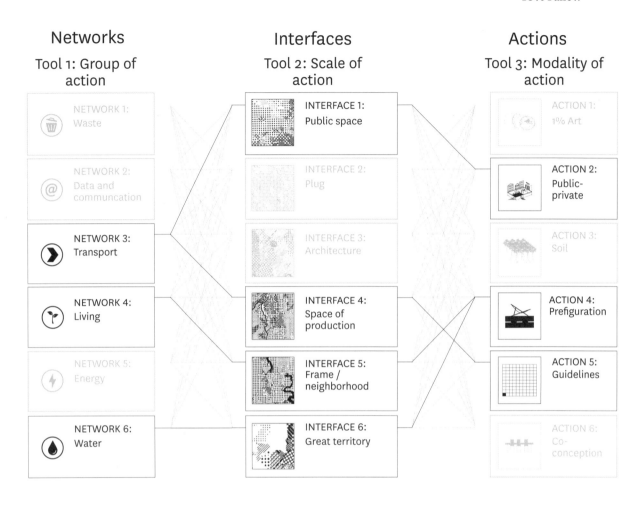

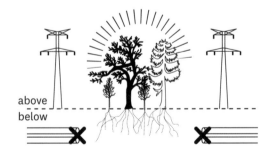

the "limit"[33] and a methodological approach. It would make it possible to grasp the elements that would link the networks to the actions while promptly reaching the other categories.

The constitution of a project's catalog has impelled the creation of classification. The categories correspond to the three approaches associated with territorial reconfiguration:

1/ "Urban correspondences"
(urbanism+art type)
The common denominator is the assumption of the site as the center—revealing its power of action, placing

[33] Lynch, *L'image de la Cité*. "On the edge:" "des éléments linéaires du paysage urbain, susceptibles d'être parcourus visuellement et qui constituent le bord d'éléments surfaciques. Ce sont des éléments naturels ou anthropiques, qui forment de véritables ruptures à l'intérieur de la ville."

Fig. 17: Matrix of the living networks
Fig. 18: Oasis

32

it at the heart of the narration. Sponge and reactive areas favor the introduction of temporary actions, prefigurations, or urban art that initiate and embody projects that are often complex and long, sometimes pre-existing, but in need of being reintegrated into the transition.

around the emergence zone of the network, control of the land or its negotiations, and a place for a new urban strategy. By bringing together these opportunities, we regularly reach 10 percent of the territory: extra space is opposed to extinction,[34] and evasion is opposed to continuing densification. The image echoes "redemption," as well as Paul Cézanne's "white" unpainted area.[35] Fallow land compels the policy of time with its rotations of productive emptiness, which can relate to "zero net artificialization" of the ground.[36]

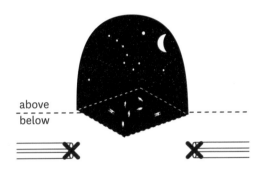

2/ "Urban fallow land"
(territory and economy type)
Decolonization of the visible by the invisible. The proposal of a reserve, a protective space to help absorb the coming shocks. We could take the image of the airbag: giving qualities to existing pockets while making them cushions against risks. It requires an enlargement of the sensitive areas

3/ "Revelation"
(architecture type, landscape architecture)
Urban revelation, the iceberg typology:[37]
the emergence of the network as an icon.

In *Wasting away*,[38] Lynch tackles the issue of waste and describes many spatial situations (along, or at the end of the network), and the emerging figures are described as places of freedom.

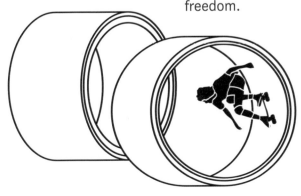

34 Banerji, *De la forêt.*
35 Handke, *La leçon de la sainte victoire.*
36 Fosse, *Objectif "Zéro artificialisation nette."*
37 Remaud, *Penser comme un iceberg.*
38 Lynch, *Wasting away.*

Fig. 19: Closure
Fig. 20: Space of freedom

III.

Territorial Habitat

Aglaée Degros

Peeing in the shower isn't enough to save the earth![1] We need something that makes far more fundamental changes to our ways of doing things if we are to address the challenges of climate change and over-consumption of resources as well as ecological impoverishment and its social consequences. We have to move from an individual commitment to these challenges to a collective responsibility. And, as a discipline that shapes the development of human settlements, urbanism has a major role to play. It is not as much about the construction of the building itself as the disposition of the buildings, their relationship, and how they are connected to the environment.[2] The question for us, as urbanists, is therefore how to make structural changes to our approach—we need to go far beyond passively witnessing the addition of small initiatives trying to cope with huge challenges. In fact, the development of the discipline is deeply linked to the Anthropocene and the dependence of our society on fossil fuels, making collective structural change all the more necessary for its survival.

[1] Narins, "Gwyneth Paltrow's Goop Encourages You to Pee in the Shower."

[2] Degros et al., *Basics of Urbanism*.

It is from the period of the "great acceleration" of the Anthropocene pollution indicator that the discipline really takes off.[3] When industrialization began, there was an influx of people into the places of production, the cities. Faced with the anarchic and unhealthy development of these cities, critical analyses, theories, and plans on the city were developed to improve the living conditions of its inhabitants. Urbanism as we know it, and therefore the art, science, and techniques that we develop to make our cities today, is a "co-lateral" consequence of the exploitation of our resources and the domination of humans over their environment.

To open the debate on the transition to be made in the discipline in order to leave a logic of production and exploitation of resources, to express doubts in relation to a problem, without having previously conceived a "solution," can be considered as stupid.[4] But acting in the name of the common good is about more than winning an argument. As such, *Towards Territorial Transition* aims to open up directions for exploration. Instead of promoting an instant solution, which leads to us formulating answers that are often quick, simple, and already proven, this book proposes slow and complex paths. It distances itself from urban planning trends that make a similar diagnosis but respond with nostalgia. Taking refuge in nostalgia is one way of

escaping from the shift that has to be made, as it is an approach providing quick answers that have already stood the test of time. Such an easy way out only isolates the discipline from a society confronted with the complexity of ecological and social crises and the transition to be made. Not daring to face the problems head on and make fundamental changes means ignoring the discipline's societal and spatial responsibilities.

Taking refuge in nostalgia is one way of escaping from the shift that has to be made, as it is an approach providing quick answers that have already stood the test of time.

And our responsibilities are many. Architecture professor Brian Cody recently made the blunt statement that the only problem with urbanism is speculation,[5] as the built environment has become an economic value rather than a response to the need to inhabit. Although this statement is quite simple, it nevertheless illustrates the extreme lack of societal responsibility in the discipline, which uncritically accepts the consumption of resources not with the aim of inhabiting but of treasuring a capital. The urbanist responds to questions of spatial planning with buildings, whether or not they meet an essential need, and

3 Depaule, Castex, and Panerai, *Formes urbaines de l'îlot à la barre.*

4 Macy, "Agir avec le désespoir environnemental."

5 Cody, *Personal Communication.*

spatializes capital without considering whether this is truly necessary. Our responsibility with regard to the consumption of resources thus appears to be forgotten.

The urbanist responds to questions of spatial planning with buildings, whether or not they meet an essential need, and spatializes capital without considering whether this is truly necessary.

To ask the question of the paradigmatic change within the discipline towards an "inhabited territory" and not a "speculated territory" without knowing the answers brings us closer to the real societal challenges even if the argument is still not won.

Territory is an ambiguous concept—it is both geopolitical, almost military, and at the same time perceived as a set of essential systems that allow us to live, such as water, energy, or food. Urbanism should therefore be based on the understanding of the complex dynamics of these systems.[6] This then needs to lead towards their gradual transformation into resource-saving or regenerating systems. And to the spatialization of the transformations. For decades we have accumulated "stuff" and by extension buildings, thinking that their possession and accumulation brings us closer to prosperity, without being aware of the limits of resources. Our consumption of the world is now endangering our well-being and that of future generations. Economist Tim Jackson[7] explains that we need to

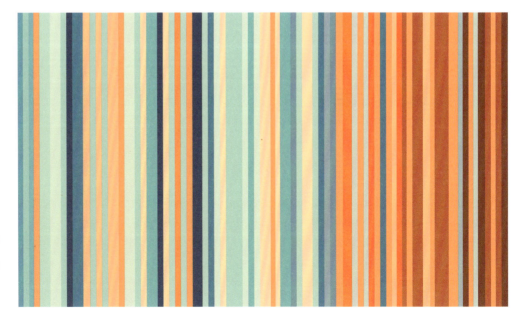

6 Bertalanffy, *General System Theory*.
7 Jackson, *Prosperity without Growth*.

Fig. 21: Warming stripes

stop associating growth with prosperity. He invites us to invent a model where our aspiration to live a good life is compatible with the limitations and constraints of a planet with limited resources. Surprisingly, frugality or reducing our desires to basic needs is not austere or depressing because one of our basic needs is in fact to live in a beautiful environment.[8]

To achieve a beautiful environment, we must therefore dare to set limits on our consumption. Here, limitation should not be seen as an obstacle to prosperity but as one of its foundations. In nature there are clear limits: between day and night, winter and summer; these limits are taken for granted and even used as a basis for organization. Nowadays, in urban planning, boundaries are seen as a hindrance to individual happiness, which is overvalued. Recently, a community living on the periphery of

> He invites us to invent a model where our aspiration to live a good life is compatible with the limitations and constraints of a planet with limited resources.

[8] Goutal, *Être Écoféministe*.

Fig. 22: Large-scale green-blue corridors – main square in Sint Niklaas, Belgium

Fig. 23: Grote Markt Sint-Niklaas green network

Territorial Habitat

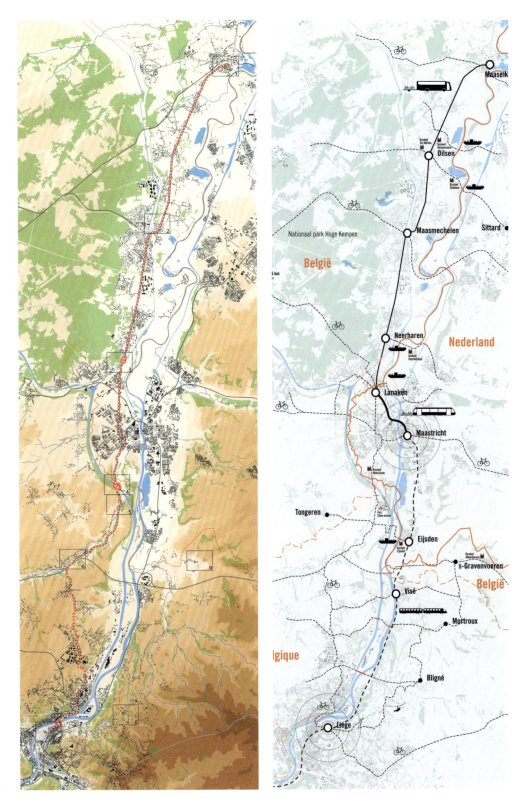

Fig. 24: Spooronderzoek map

Montreal expressed its distress about the transformation of its environment. This area is characterized by its remarkable trees, but every time a plot of land is purchased built volumes multiply to the detriment of the environment, transforming the neighborhood into a heat island and taking away its beauty. The felling of trees is not limited and is subordinated to the individual need for an increasing amount of building space. Whereas in the 1970s a person needed 20m^2 of living space, today that same person needs 40m^2.[9] In view of the pressure on the ecological system, individual building volumes should be questioned. The value of the collective is often not perceived or is perceived as a necessary evil to support the individual. The street is seen as a passageway infrastructure giving access to individual plots and not as a space in its own right which can have value and represent a societal project.

Now, the increasing individual consumption of land is jeopardizing collective well-being (present and future) by reducing natural space and expending resources.

Now, the increasing individual consumption of land is jeopardizing collective well-being (present and future) by reducing natural space and expending resources. Shouldn't we redefine certain limits that allow us to live well without hindering the lives of others, both now and in the future? Shouldn't we set limits that favor the

[9] Leclercq and Sabbah, "Loger Mobile. Sans Tourner En Rond."

Fig. 25: *T.OP Noordrand*

Territorial Habitat

community if we want to achieve our environmental objectives? Shouldn't we limit the consumption of land through the construction of buildings in order to create a real habitat?

This difference between buildings and habitat is consciously ignored in urbanism. To inhabit is to be part of an environment rather than to transform it; it is to be part of an ecological system without necessarily dominating it. Habitats are, for example, not unique to humans—animals also have a habitat. In her speech on living cities, philosopher Chris Younès associates "the viable, the livable and the equitable."[10] She invites us to set up "devices of alliance and metabolisms between humans and non-humans, solidarities and cross-breeding, cooperation, landscape continuities and hybridizations, these different natural-cultural resiliencies do not remain a simple juxtaposition in peaceful relations." Finally, she proposes the rediscovery of the symbiosis between humans and the environment, and more-than-humans. The Territorial Habitat transforms the subsistence systems of humans, such as water and energy, but also gives space to non-humans. This invites us to set up coalitions of territorial agents able to represent other interests than those of consumption.[11] The philosopher Joëlle Zask invites us to rethink the relationship between man and environment in her books *Quand la forêt brule* and *Zoocities*.[12] For her, the city as we know it has historically been conceived against nature and as protection from wild animals. To welcome these animals among us seems unthinkable. To reject them,

[10] Younès, *Europan Lecture*.
[11] Reed, and Lister, *Projective Ecologies*.
[12] Zask, *Quand la forêt brûle*.

Fig. 26: Kaiser-Franz-Josef-Kai Graz before
Fig. 27: Kaiser-Franz-Josef-Kai Graz under construction
Fig. 28: Towards carbon neutral mobility – visualization of Kaiser-Franz-Josef-Kai Graz

Territorial Habitat

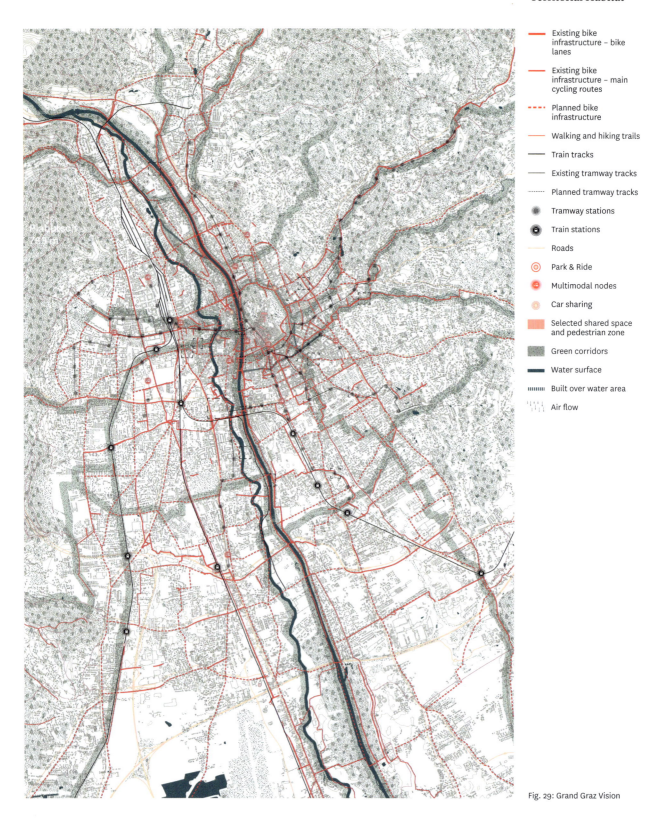

Fig. 29: Grand Graz Vision

42

Territorial Habitat

For her, the city as we know it has historically been conceived against nature and as protection from wild animals. To welcome these animals among us seems unthinkable. To reject them, impossible. To exterminate them, cruel and dangerous for the ecological balance. Her publication asks us what a city would look like in which distances and spaces would make it possible to coexist with wild animals. She asks what sort of city would no longer be designed against animals, nor for them, but with them.

Fig. 30: Grand Graz Ungergasse before
Fig. 31: Grand Graz Ungergasse after
Fig. 32: Grand Graz Elisabethinergasse before
Fig. 33: Grand Graz Elisabethinergasse after

This absence of dichotomy between humans and nature with its animals and plants, makes us think of archaic worlds. Prompted by the pandemic and its accompanying confinement, Latour proposes a new approach to our environment in his book "Où suis je?":[13] that of becoming terrestrial. Being limited to our locality made us rediscover our immediate environment; all of a sudden we put down our suitcases as global citizens and opened our eyes to what we have done with the earth that surrounds us. We rediscovered walks, local holidays, farmer's markets, and parks. Encouraging these discoveries to be translated into a revalorization of the earth, Latour proposes making "Earth a credible base." Looking closely, it is clear that there will be work to do and that we will have to roll up our sleeves. We will have to seriously abandon modernity, and its anchorage in progress and unlimited growth. Making the city no longer involves planning as a master in the style of Le Corbusier when he proposed his Plan Voisin; instead, it means taking on the role of WALL-E in the film of the same name, who, on his mission to clear "urban stuff" by chance discovers a small green plant—a sign of a possible future.

To adopt this approach is to take care of the environment, the earth; it is to be terrestrial. The difficulty is all the greater because all these terms of "soil," "territory," "people," "tradition," "earth" and "return to the earth," "anchoring," "localization," and "organicity" have all been appropriated, colonized by modernity to describe the past, the archaic, the reactionary, which had to be torn away from at all costs by a formidable push towards the future.

Looking closely, it is clear that there will be work to do and that we will have to roll up our sleeves. We will have to seriously abandon modernity, and its anchorage in progress and unlimited growth.

To take them up again is to cover oneself with the tunic of Nessus. And the burn stings all the more because these same terms have been claimed, this time positively, by those who have indeed accepted going back, finding the protection of a homeland, of a nation, of a soil, of a people, of an ethnic group, of a past dream. "If globalization leads nowhere, they cry out, at least give us a safe place to live, confined perhaps, but protected and above all among ourselves."[14] How can we make it "light" and not reactionary valorize to the earth? To be terrestrial would mean not being modern, no longer thinking of the city as a set of buildings, infrastructures, and functions. Not to be conservative and to refer to the historical city and its nostalgia, not to build, but to inhabit.

13 Latour, *Où suis-je?*
14 Idem.

Territorial Habitat

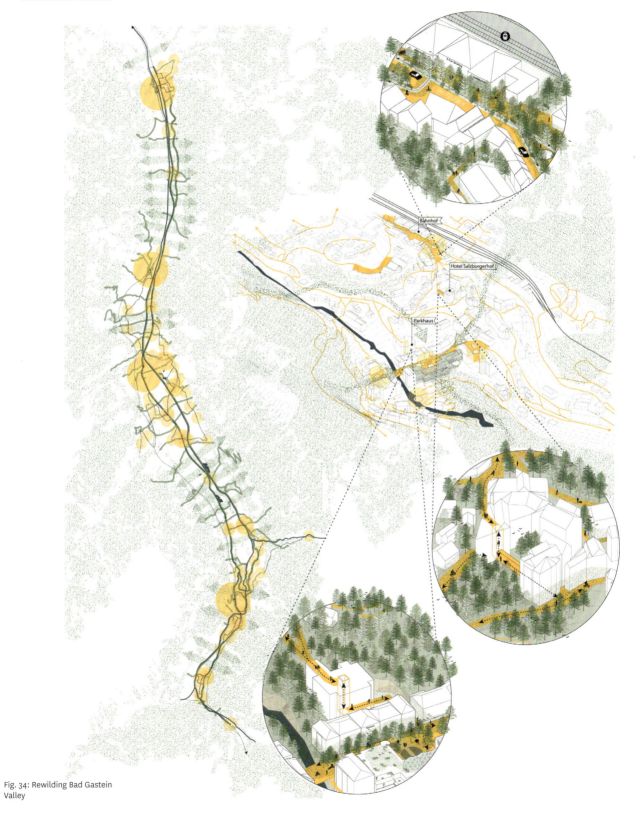

Fig. 34: Rewilding Bad Gastein Valley

45

In urbanism, the current question is thus how to design an inhabited territory without being reactionary. There is no return to the candle or the carrier pigeon, but rather a critique of the conception of a world where humans are considered as "homo oeconomicus,"[15] and consequently the organization of economic issues is held to be the source of happiness or unhappiness in all areas. Economic growth, through industrialization and then digitalization, is the holy grail of materialism, the undisputed source from which abundance, well-being, and the evolution of society are supposed to flow.[16] But what if technologies were no longer at the service of consumerism or progress (which is increasingly based on the progressive destruction of the foundations of life[17]) and were instead used to increase quality of life and respond to fundamental needs?[18] Technology can help optimize the use or regeneration of resources, for example by reducing the amount of space consumed. The focus here could be on "space saving," reducing the footprint of buildings (by recycling them), reducing the surface area given over to traffic, reducing the sealing of space by spatially optimizing systems—while aiming to offer the claimed space to nature. One example would be optimizing the interstitial space between the built-up areas, space that for a long

time has simply been neglected and considered to have no ecological value or potential, leading to it being wasted. It is often used for traffic, or for profitable functions and filled with stuff, but rarely considered as a space with high natural potential for transformation. Yet it is precisely this interstitial space that allows the location of ecological networks, such as water and vegetation. For this spatialization to be possible, its value must be recognized, and it must be shared equitably through possible technological changes.

The focus here could be on "space saving," reducing the footprint of buildings (by recycling them), reducing the surface area given over to traffic, reducing the sealing of space by spatially optimizing systems—while aiming to offer the claimed space to nature.

We need to reconsider the place of technology, progress, and modernity; we need to question the norm. It seems impossible to imagine the world without the Anthropocene and its modernity, but it was preceded by other age-old norms. Our current routines ensure our comfort, but is comfort really the same as quality of life?

15 Spretnak, *The Resurgence of the Real.*

16 Goutal, *Être Écoféministe.*

17 Shiva, Mies, and Salleh, *Ecofeminism.*

18 Fehrenbach and Recki, *Natur und Technik*

Do we value our comfort so highly that we are happy to pay for it by endangering our children's future? One must dare to move beyond comfort, questioning some of the modern evidence and becoming avant-garde in the French sense of the word as Panos Mantziaras of the Braillard Foundation in charge of the transition of Luxembourg explains that "Avant-garde is the one who is sent before the guard and who often sacrifices himself!"[19]

Our current routines ensure our comfort, but is comfort really the same as quality of life?

The norm must be replaced by a process where quality is ensured by the negotiation of the agents representing the systems. This mechanism is more flexible in terms of both time and context, allowing for the absorption of uncertainties.

If peeing in the shower is not enough, we need to understand hydraulic and waste systems, to transform them into more efficient and frugal systems. We must dare to be stupid! We must try to involve the agents who carry out this transformation at all scales, developing platforms involving those agents and being responsible for its spatialization of systems. This could fundamentally change our understanding of urbanism and perhaps even save the earth.

19 Panos, "Territorial Design in Geneva and Luxembourg."

IV.

Territorial Atlas

In the Territorial Atlas of Luxembourg, various layers of infrastructures and data were superimposed in order to understand their complex interrelationships. The networks of the Luxembourg metropolitan area that emerged from the superposition show how spatial disruptions, anomalies, and other deviations of the territory translate spatially, climatically, economically, or socially. The previously segregated areas of settlement have merged into a continuum. The hinterland has disappeared or become part of the urban center. Instead of individual settlement types, the territory is now defined by an interstitial landscape of more or less coherent networks.

Three major insights emerged from the iterative, exploratory reading of the atlas: 1) Hybridization and possible synergies between networks, 2) Physical-spatial organization of the networks and their location in relation to the ground, and 3) Priority of the networks as a resource.

Atlas methodology

The cartographic scale of the cross-border "functional region" of the Luxembourg metropolitan area is represented to describe the networks and their reciprocal interactions. The major infrastructure corridors with their accompanying ecologically valuable green spaces create spatial discontinuities in the landscape. These define the system boundaries of the intervention, that is, the new working perimeter that encompasses the real functional metropolis. These new boundaries of functional and eco-systemic networks deviate spatially from the administrative boundaries and blur Luxembourg's border areas with its neighboring countries.

The first objective was to identify the relevant data. This step was followed by the creation of surveys defined by both geographic determinants and the maximum extent of the infrastructural networks under study. This atlas is synoptic and allows for the representation of the networks in the Luxembourg metropolitan area.

Network atlas—risk map and layers
Although Luxembourg has historically been characterized by the spread of forests throughout the country, a 2019 study surveyed their health and found that only 13.4% of trees are in good condition. The predicted climatic extremes pose an enormous threat not only to large-scale infrastructures, but in particular to green forest corridors as networks.

Eighteen investigation sites are located in spatial relation to the hazard zones in order to critically explore the potential risks. The aim here is to reveal and anticipate future changes and adaptations. Most of them are affected by major floods. The samples are organized into six themes related to six system typologies (water, waste, energy, transportation, housing, digital). Another six project-based approaches allow for the analysis of different themes both general and specific to the Luxembourg territory, such as transboundary management, hyper-nature, icebergs, platforms, regulation, temporary actions, and land economy.

This leads to a systematic reflection on the strategic action levels, such as building, street, public space, neighborhood, production site, and territory. Three perimeters of 100, 1000 and 10,000 hectares are defined, making it possible to find the most appropriate scale depending on the site studied.

Territorial Atlas

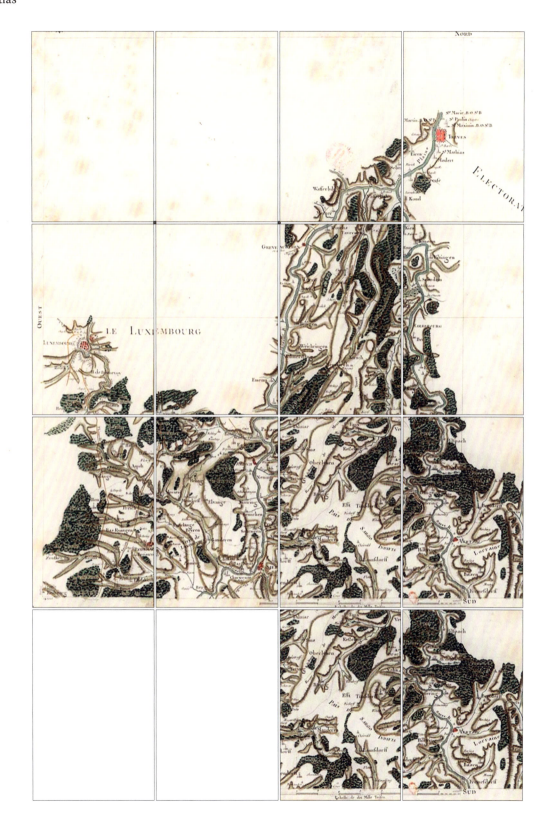

Fig. 35: Map of France by order of the King, 1763

51

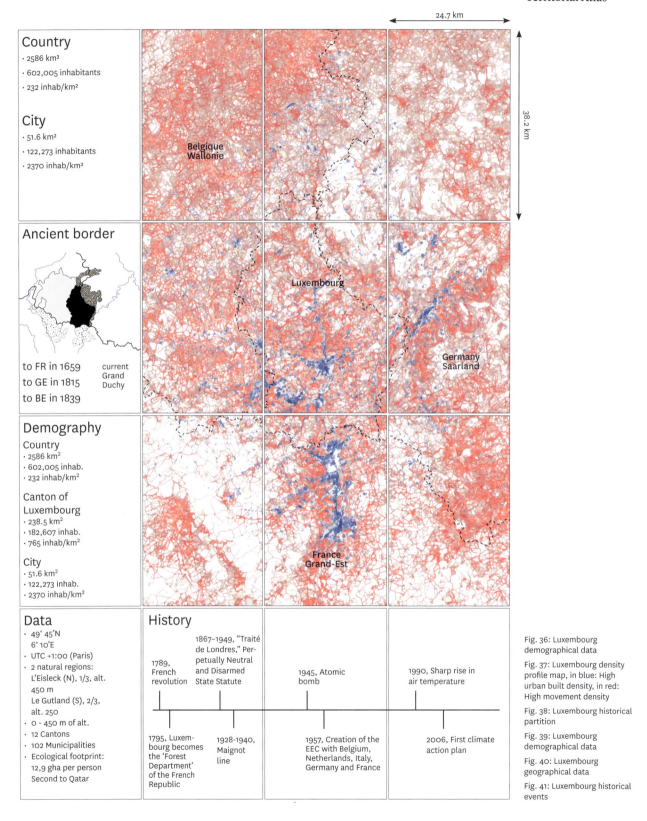

Fig. 36: Luxembourg demographical data

Fig. 37: Luxembourg density profile map, in blue: High urban built density, in red: High movement density

Fig. 38: Luxembourg historical partition

Fig. 39: Luxembourg demographical data

Fig. 40: Luxembourg geographical data

Fig. 41: Luxembourg historical events

Territorial Atlas

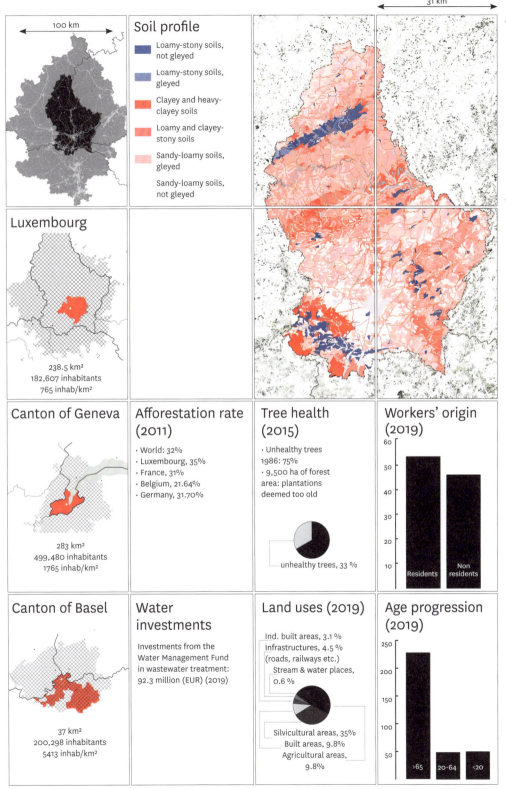

Fig. 42: Luxembourg and its border regions
Fig. 43: Soil profile map and legend
Fig. 44: Territories comparison
Fig. 45: Afforestation rate quantity
Fig. 46: Territories comparison
Fig. 47: Tree health quantity
Fig. 48: Employment quantity
Fig. 49: Territories comparison
Fig. 50: Water investment quantity
Fig. 51: Land uses quantity
Fig. 52: Demographical quantity

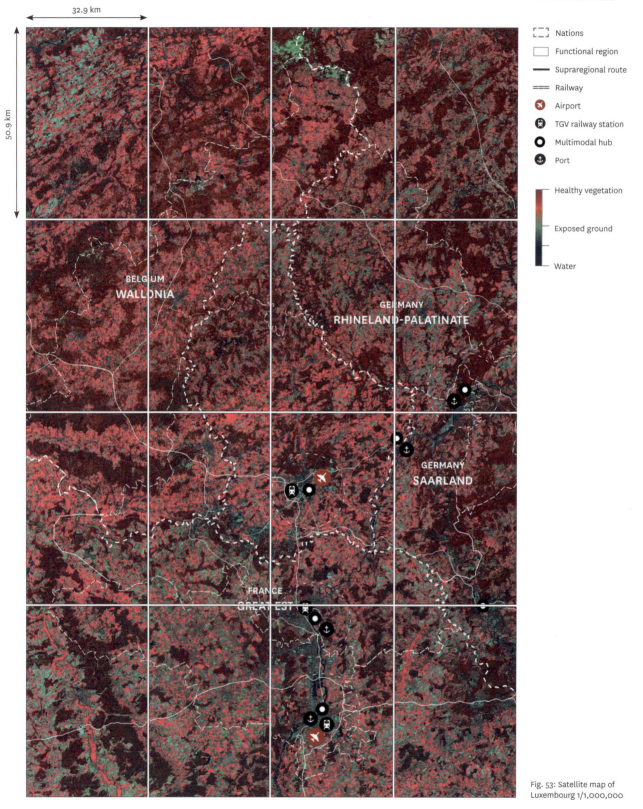

Fig. 53: Satellite map of Luxembourg 1/1,000,000

Territorial Atlas

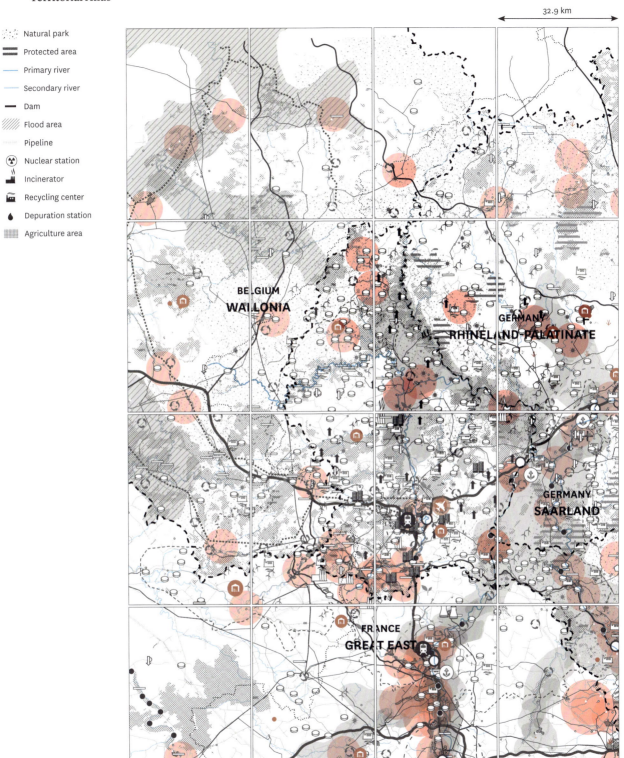

Fig. 54: Territorial analysis of the six network interrelations 1/1,000,000

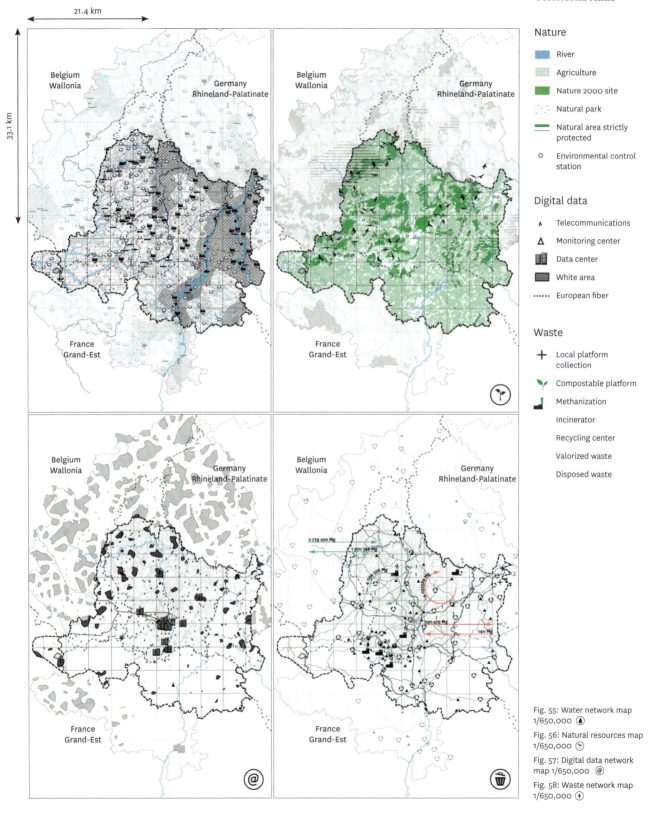

Territorial Atlas

Risk

- ▨ Flood zones
- ▨ High risk
- ▨ Medium risk
- ▨ Low risk
- ☢ Nuclear station
- - - - Nuclear radius
  5-10-20 km

Energy

- Nuclear
- Wind power
- Solar
- Gasifier
- Methanizer
- Hydraulic
- Combustion

Renewable energy
production (MV/km²)

- 0-200
- 200-400
- 400-600
- 600+

Transport

- —— Supra-regional roads
- —— Intra-regional roads
- ▦ Railway
- —— Waterways
- ✈ Airport
- Air cargo platform
- ◎ Multimodal hub
- ⚓ Port
- TGV train station

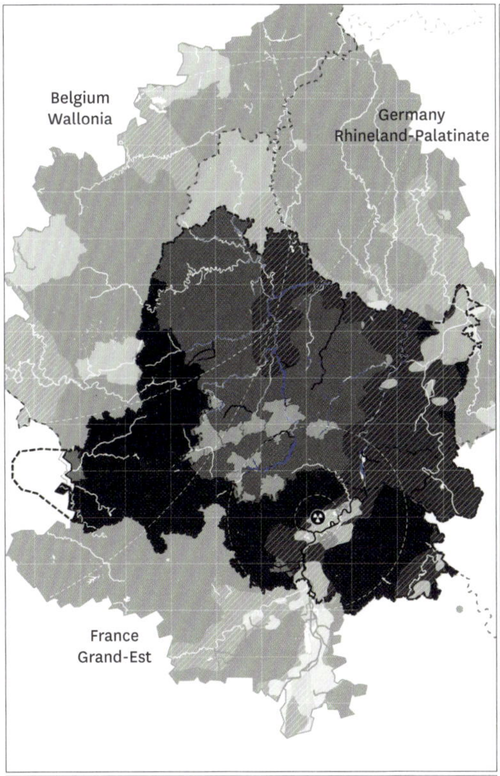

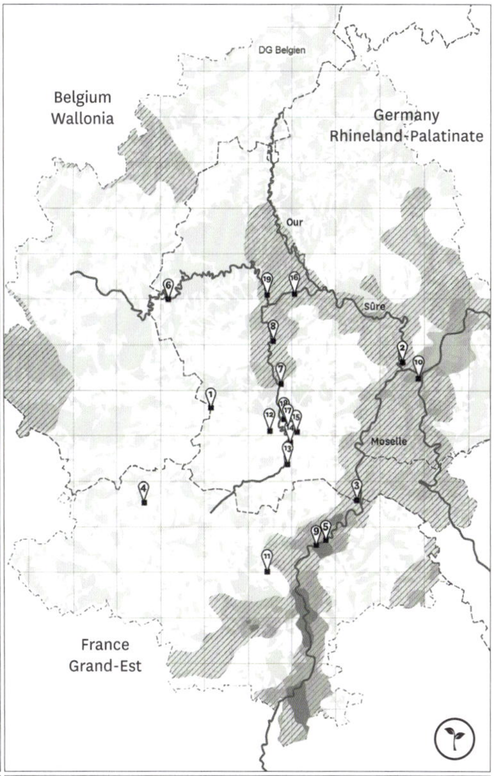

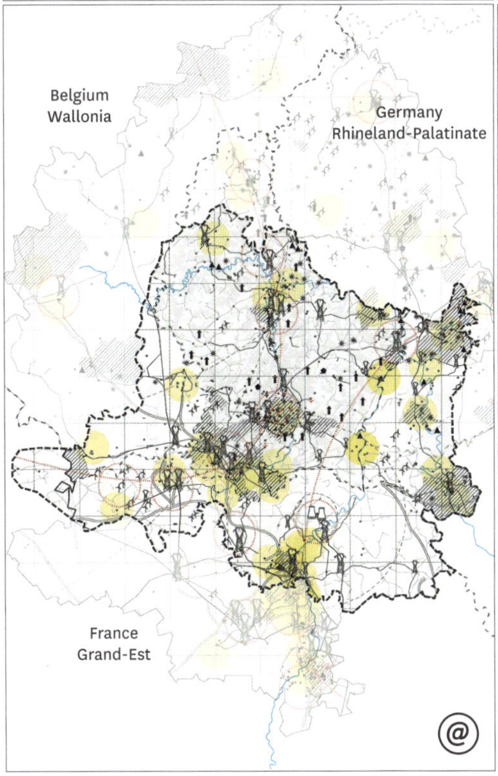

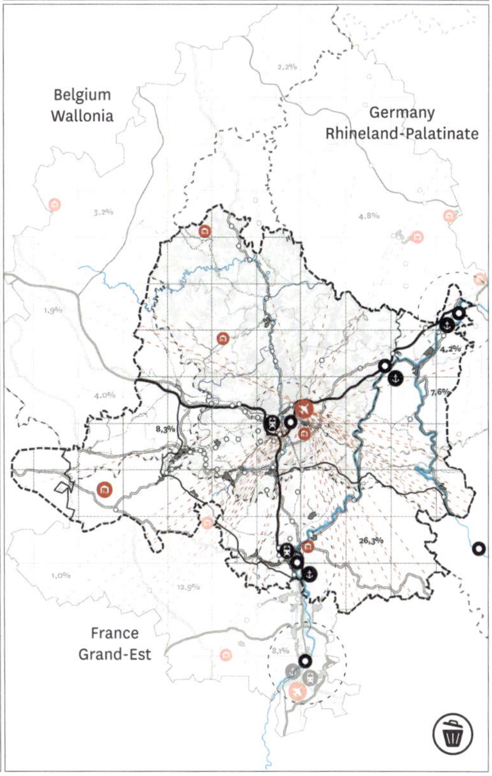

Fig. 59: Natural risk map
1/650,000

Fig. 60: Flood water and tree
health status map 1/650,000

Fig. 61: Energy network map
1/650,000 ⊕

Fig. 62: Transport network
map 1/650,000 ❯

57

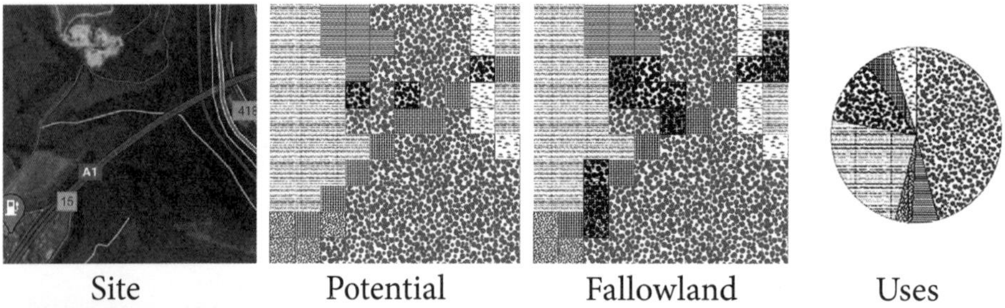

Territorial Atlas

Site	Potential	Fallowland	Uses		

Network infrastructure 5%
River 5%
Forest 46%
Quarry 5%
Marshes 0%
Buildings 3%
Fields 24%
Fallow 12%

Fig. 63: Site 01 analysis

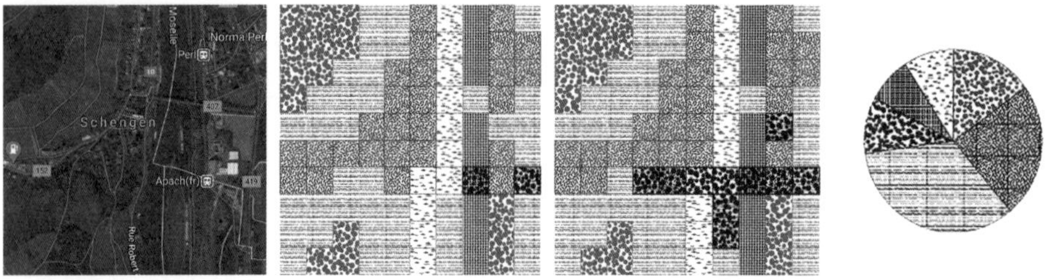

Network infrastructure 8%
River 9%
Forest 15%
Quarry 0%
Marshes 0%
Buildings 24%
Fields 34%
Fallow 10%

Fig. 64: Site 02 analysis

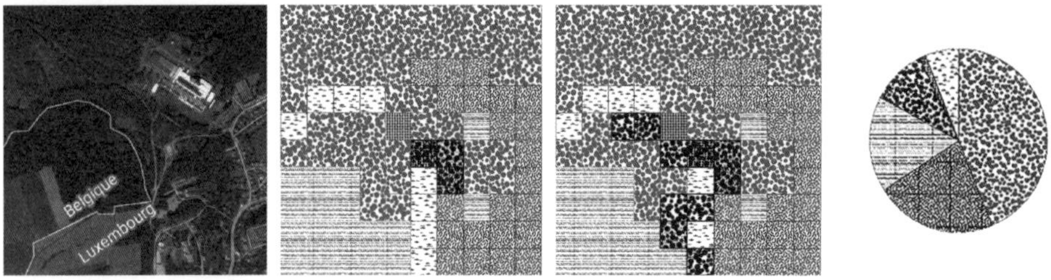

Network infrastructure 1%
River 6%
Forest 44%
Quarry 0%
Marshes 0%
Buildings 22%
Fields 17%
Fallow 10%

Fig. 65: Site 03 analysis

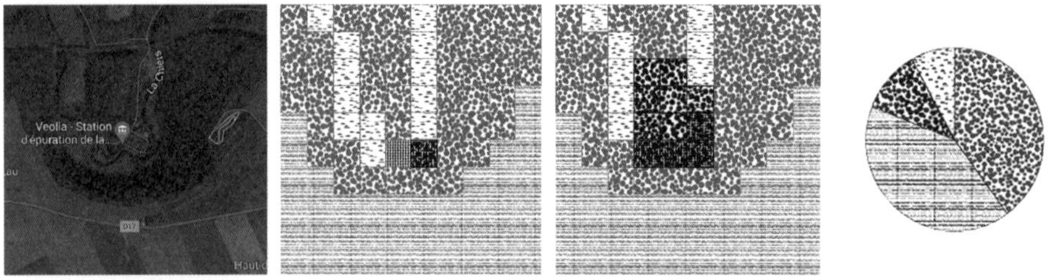

Network infrastructure 0%
River 8%
Forest 40%
Quarry 0%
Marshes 0%
Buildings 0%
Fields 41%
Fallow 11%

Fig. 66: Site 04 analysis

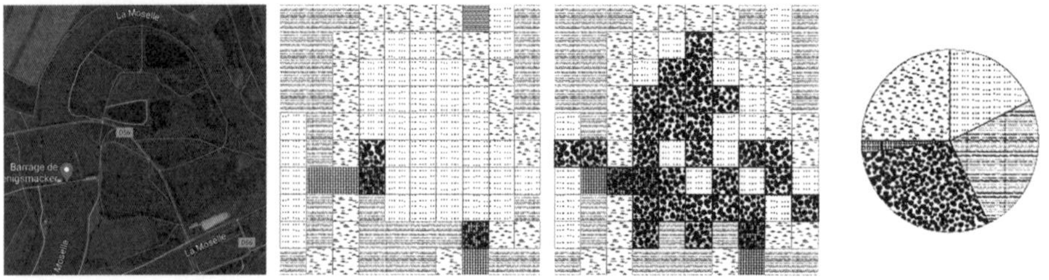

Network infrastructure 2%
River 25%
Forest 0%
Quarry 0%
Marshes 18%
Buildings 0%
Fields 25%
Fallow 30%

Fig. 67: Site 05 analysis

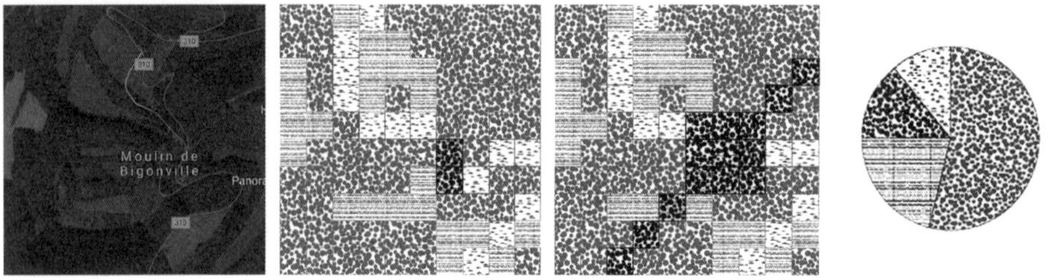

Network infrastructure 0%
River 11%
Forest 54%
Quarry 0%
Marshes 0%
Buildings 0%
Fields 21%
Fallow 14%

Fig. 68: Site 06 analysis

Territorial Atlas

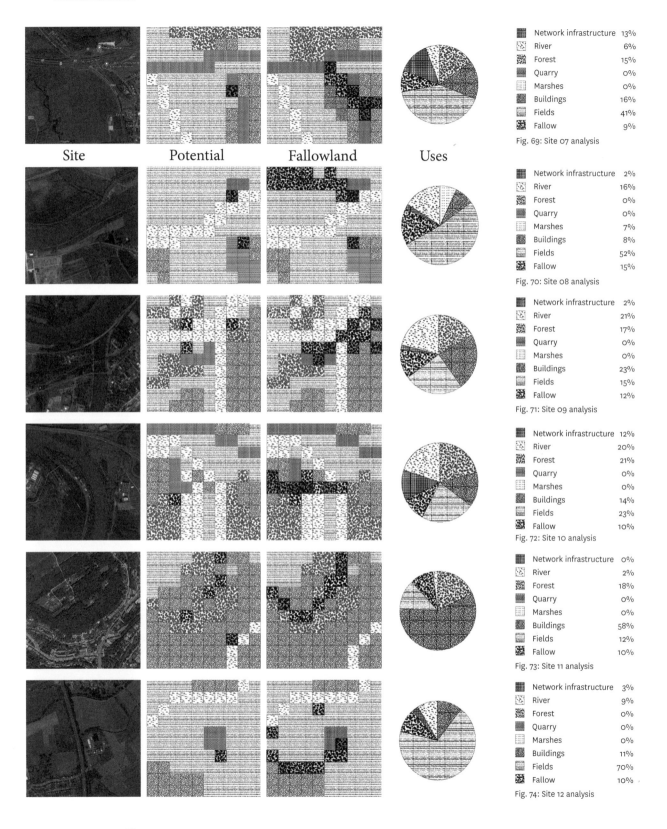

Site　Potential　Fallowland　Uses

Network infrastructure	13%	
River	6%	
Forest	15%	
Quarry	0%	
Marshes	0%	
Buildings	16%	
Fields	41%	
Fallow	9%	

Fig. 69: Site 07 analysis

Network infrastructure	2%
River	16%
Forest	0%
Quarry	0%
Marshes	7%
Buildings	8%
Fields	52%
Fallow	15%

Fig. 70: Site 08 analysis

Network infrastructure	2%
River	21%
Forest	17%
Quarry	0%
Marshes	0%
Buildings	23%
Fields	15%
Fallow	12%

Fig. 71: Site 09 analysis

Network infrastructure	12%
River	20%
Forest	21%
Quarry	0%
Marshes	0%
Buildings	14%
Fields	23%
Fallow	10%

Fig. 72: Site 10 analysis

Network infrastructure	0%
River	2%
Forest	18%
Quarry	0%
Marshes	0%
Buildings	58%
Fields	12%
Fallow	10%

Fig. 73: Site 11 analysis

Network infrastructure	3%
River	9%
Forest	0%
Quarry	0%
Marshes	0%
Buildings	11%
Fields	70%
Fallow	10%

Fig. 74: Site 12 analysis

V.

Territorial Portrait

Anna Positano

The photo essay makes visible the relation between planning paradigms, climate change, society, and territory. With her photographic study of everyday places, Anna Positano provides an atmospheric visual perspective on the narration of lives, both human and more-than-human.

The photo essay expresses the complexity and uncertainties of anthropocentric landscapes in transition. It reports on Luxembourg in 2021 and its massive hazard risks but also the spatial consequences that arise from the climate urgency. The essay addresses the planning practices and protocols that are still strongly related to high carbon emissions and resource consumption.

VI.

Round Table

Territorial transition is neither a phenomenon, idea, aim, nor a tool but a long-term process. It is a network of complex relations between territory, scale, resources, platforms, uncertainty, and transition. Starting from these six notions, different professionals, such as urbanists, architects, and landscape architects immersed themselves in a conversation that reveals the critical metrics, strategies, and processes needed for the territorial transition.

The round table conversation explores different approaches to territorial transition that critically address disciplinary boundaries, the elasticity of consumption-related territories, the understanding of the client in transition design, and the right to climate adaptation. The members of the panel were:

Anita Berrizbeitia **(AB)**

Panos Mantziaras **(PM)**

Matthias Armengaud **(MA)**

Aglaée Degros **(AD)**

Radostina Radulova-Stahmer **(RR)**
Moderator of the round table

PM: Ecological transition is a term that was used as early as the seventies, primarily gaining traction through John W. Bennett's seminal book *The Ecological Transition* (1976). This book showed an early and remarkably accurate understanding of transition. However, in 1987, the Brundtland Report was published and the term of sustainable development took over, meaning that transition as a concept was not pursued further by scientists.

The term sustainable development became a political term in the mid-eighties and remained dominant until the beginning of 2010, having gained importance in the scientific community. However, it stayed in the realm of the sciences, things only changing when it was connected to the idea of energy transition, as in the ground-breaking book *Transition Handbook, from oil dependency to local resilience* (2008) written by Transition Towns Movement founder Rob Hopkins. However, all this time the ecological transition as an overall concept stayed in the background. It became easier to address once there was a clear focus on energy, as the transition from fossil fuel energies to alternative renewable energies seems more specific and manageable. Generally, the idea behind it is that the Anthropocene and the fossil economy are closely related, as it is the fossil economy which is behind the specific Anthropocene situation. This is a phenomenon where we observe the human capacity to permanently alter the face of the earth in a non-reversible way. What is interesting about the ecological transition is that it is a project (to transit from point A to point B) within a phenomenon (the Anthropocene). Thus, in the context of the global Anthropocene era, around the year 2000, we started moving towards the goal of long-term sustainable development in a non-fossil economy.

In this sense, the ecological transition is not infinite. It is very specific in time; it has a beginning (now) and an end at a point where humanity will live in a non-fossil fuel economy, within a zero-carbon society.

In this sense, the ecological transition is not infinite. It is very specific in time; it has a beginning (now) and an end at a point where humanity will live in a non-fossil fuel economy, within a zero-carbon society. Transition needs to be quantified; it needs a metric. There might be other ways to talk about transition but these are not precise enough and therefore not helpful.

In academia the transition is really not mainstream if you look at what is circulating in the announcements of conferences and colloquiums in Europe or the US. Not even 10 percent are on this question.

AB: In the US we don't talk about it as transition. We just say carbon-neutral. Nobody is thinking of it as a process; the focus lies on the result. That's a big mistake.

MA: How can we use the term transition? Is it a dynamic tool for a project, or is it a poetic word?

Nobody is thinking of it as a process; the focus lies on the result. That's a big mistake.

AB: It is clear that we need a transition, despite the uncertainties this will bring, as we are faced with ecological and environmental urgencies and we are now seeing the impacts of them in every country and every area of the world. And with them economic vulnerabilities also emerge. We have to think of the transition as a project that will address environmental and socio-economic vulnerabilities. I like how you say that the ecological transition has a time frame. We have a goal which is to change into a post-fossil fuel economy and that is a tangible aim. The issue for us as designers is the domino effect that impacts the environment. This is where we as architects and landscape architects, planners, and urban designers work. We are not only very interested in the impact of the ecological transition but in the wide-reaching effect of all of this. That suggests that transition itself becomes a design project, rather than the endpoint. The process of designing is defined by the client, the time frame, and the budget. But designing is also a way of predicting the domino effect and redirecting it towards a broader set of concerns—we no longer want to be duplicating the mono-functionality of any landscape or infrastructural intervention. A further question is how can we do more with less? How can we not only predict unexpected consequences, but redirect the causal sequence for other purposes, such as flood mitigation, climate adaptation, or the creation of alternative kinds of economies, etc. We need to move away from a singular approach that leads to a single solution and towards being a lot smarter now and understanding the domino effect and its possible predictable consequences.

Fig. 75: Anita Berrizbeitia

PLATFORM

MA: We need to pursue an approach characterized by plurality rather than singularity when dealing with the transition.

Does being in transition mean that we need to work as part of a cross- and multi-disciplinary platform? Panos, you have organized large-scale interdisciplinary competitions in Europe. So you have seen many teams with their own particular reflections and approaches to discussing the topic of transition. Do we need to adapt our way of working and designing as architects in order to learn about transition? Or would we need to create a specific "eco-centric" dynamic that could shift what architecture is per se?

PM: In my position as the Head of the Architectural, Urban and Landscape Research Office at the French Ministry of Culture, I was interested in American research about the disciplinary network and connections between disciplines revealed by scientific references. We asked the researchers to produce a new network graphic, incorporating architecture, which was missing from their initial studies. The result was that architecture found itself at the margin of the disciplinary universe—a sort of exo-planet—related only to literature, history, and classical studies. We were particularly surprised, because we were running the Greater Paris competition at that time, and we assumed that architecture would be closely related to engineering, ecology, economics, etc. We thus understood that interdisciplinary approaches needed to relocate architecture from the periphery to the

center of the network, strengthening its connection to economics, management, political science, etc.

The result was that architecture found itself at the margin of the disciplinary universe—a sort of exo-planet—related only to literature, history, and classical studies.

Since then, I have been endeavoring to move architecture in the direction of these new questions on the ecological transition through specific tenders, such as the one for *Luxembourg in Transition* or the Grand Geneva Consultations, basing these on what we learnt from the earlier tender for "Grand Paris" in 2008.

Fig. 76: Panos Mantziaras

The challenge is that architectural methods are still very "impressionist," which means imprecise. They are only understood by other architects. The network graphics show that scientists from different disciplines are able to understand each other and communicate. To create an interdisciplinary field means to go from a discipline to a disciplinary field.

Do we need to adapt our way of working and designing as architects in order to learn about transition? Or would we need to create a specific "eco-centric" dynamic that could shift what architecture is per se?

To do so we need to become clearly understandable to other areas. Otherwise we will remain limited by our discipline's boundaries.

AB: You have brought up a very interesting point, which leads on to post-disciplinarity. We are entering a post-disciplinary moment. The problems we are facing are very large and complex. We can no longer offer fragmented answers. Now, the problems are globally interwoven. This means we need to change the way we answer them, the constellation, and complexity. We need to think about how the complexity in the approach could be translated into the material and spatial world.

The discipline has always tackled topics on the periphery.

If you think of a Venn diagram, there has always been the core disciplinary knowledge that we are all responsible for. And as educators we have to pass on this knowledge. But when we think about the present moment it is clear we need to expand and redefine design to stay relevant, and be clear about what it is we bring to the table that others don't or can't. Are we talking about the Venn diagram being turned inside out? Could the multi-disciplinarity then be the core? And what used to be the core is the specialization?

SCALE

MA: Talking about how to turn the multi-disciplinarity into the core, Anita, you question the geographic scale of the landscape. In the *Luxembourg in Transition* process you pointed out the significance of the structure in a metropolis. Whether there is a center, a polycentric structure with its strengths, or whether you're focusing on the periphery and the hinterland with its agricultural areas. The specific landscape of Luxembourg and the surrounding countries is extremely interesting because it always combines the periphery and the center. This mix is very intriguing. The figure of the archipelago is present with a multiplicity of blurred objects. The question of Euro-scale therefore emerges.

Is there any Euro-metropolis transcending borders that we could study and that would help us to find tools to add to the transition?

AB: The question is what is the unit of research in our analysis and how does this relate to the various scales of our interventions. When you speak about city center versus periphery, those are very specific categories and typologies that demand certain questions. One clear unit of analysis is the watershed. So many of the political problems are emerging from that scale, especially when different nations, regions, and municipalities—different political or administrative units—share a watershed and their actions are not coordinated. The examples are everywhere. Other scales to look at are habitat, ecosystem structures, and, of course, energy resources. Ultimately, we also have to understand how all of these fit together; nothing exists in isolation. A related question is how elastic the concept of territory is in terms of scale. How large can it get and how small? When does it stop being territory and become something else? Our economic reach (in Luxembourg and many other countries) has a global footprint. It depends on abstract flows of capital and information at a global scale that are so much larger than the real physical territory of the country and yet, as we saw, have real repercussions in the

country that are important to understand and measure. If you draw the different territories of Luxembourg, their economy is not contained within their physical territory. That to me is interesting. How do we begin to take all this into account in our decision making as designers? And how do we address the connection between the economic base of a country and its physical territory?

The rupturing of networks, of standards, of planned tropisms shifts the perception of territories so that they are seen as fertile, valuable bodies.

MA: Panos, did organizing the large competitions provide an answer to the question of the correct unit? A Euro transborder region seems to be one possibility.

Fig. 77 Matthias Armengaud

Round Table

The rupturing of networks, of standards, of planned tropisms shifts the perception of territories so that they are seen as fertile, valuable bodies. Would a new site coherence allow for the emergence of units related to a new metric?

PM: What is a metric? A metric is a combination of elementary units. Speed is a metric because it is miles per hour. So, if you combine two units it becomes a metric. Metrics and units have been used for a long time to allow people to have a common understanding of problems. Time zones emerged around 1890, due to time conflict of the stock exchange: one opened while another one was closing. Time was a problem.

Time zones emerged around 1890, due to time conflict of the stock exchange: one opened while another one was closing. Time was a problem.

And now if we agree that CO_2 emissions are a problem we will find a metric that leads to a solution. This metric will contain CO_2 equivalents somehow. As architects, we should be able to handle the metric CO_2 per square meter if a client asks us to build a house with no more than a certain amount per square meter. From there we can calculate the footage, the size, and the CO_2

emissions globally. This is something we will come up with in the next twenty years, for sure. How can we organize our construction so we can reach the necessary scale in order to tackle wicked problems and uncertainties? The question is now how to deal with the urgency. We are now aware that the transition and CO_2 neutrality have to be reached much faster than would be the case if we left it to academics and politicians. There is a kind of countdown that we are fighting against. We now need to tackle the situation from a legal perspective.

RESOURCES

AB: What that suggests to me is that we are going from a metrical consumption to one which is about climate and about capturing CO_2, or not producing it in the first place.

But what is the domino effect of that? Are we going to stop all construction, for example?

What alternative employment options are there, given that housing is such a huge part of the economy?

Stopping construction would lead to a real crisis in many parts of the world. Who decides on the metric? Who is left out of that decision?

TERRITORY/SCALE

AD: Anita, you approached this issue in relation to the resource, meaning that the key units are the system and the territory. Bruno Latour understands the territory as the system that sustains a person. This territory can have flexible boundaries, as one person will buy strawberries coming from Spain while the other will buy them from a local producer. This is the systemic scale. But still as designers we are responsible for space—who else would take up this responsibility? There is no contradiction between understanding the system as a whole and at the same time caring about very down-to-earth spatial solutions. Still, we have to find the right tools and scales to translate the systemic change on the ground. It would be a pity to only map out observations and not address the consequences of the transition for the space we experience on an everyday basis.

TERRITORY

MA: This is a good point. Are these systemic changes visible on the ground or not? Maybe revealing what is visible and invisible in the territory could be used as a technique to approach transition. What does the invisible mean? Do we have to reveal the unseen parts of the territory?

Part of our process design is linking networks and revealing resources.

AB: Let's also look at the question of what is stimulating the production of certain infrastructures or certain lines on the territory.

Maybe revealing what is visible and invisible in the territory could be used as a technique to approach transition.

MA: It is a strategic approach, to bring what is invisible back as a strong tool for the design project. In our master studio the students built almost nothing or very few square meters. We rather remove certain flows, combine energies, reveal invisible practices and unclear situations, or underline potentials.

AD: Our experience was that the visualizations in the master studio projects often show a society which is perpetually happy. Not only adding buildings but also improving systems can result in an increased quality of life. But are humans really at the center of a more ecological and just world?

We need to move beyond focusing on positive human emotions to communicate the value of the transformation and the added spatial quality, and instead also question humanity's role in the future.

PM: And how do we generally visually communicate the work on transition?

AB: What about designing not for people but for an endangered species? That is something that is invisible but has tangible consequences. Then certain territories, habitats, neo-landscapes will begin to emerge. We should move from a model of lifestyle consumption to a model of a good life for specific entities. It can be any endangered plant or animal, anything that is alive but is not a human. What would then happen? The problem is that our colonializing instincts are so strong we've become narrow in our agendas.

There is no similar number to aim for in terms of biodiversity, which makes it very hard for scientists to install biodiversity as part of the story about climate change. We need to be able to measure it.

PM: The question of biodiversity is very important, as is the question of how we can design for it. In a recent article in the Guardian, biodiversity scientists highlighted the problem concerning biodiversity related to climate change, calling for a metric to give people a horizon they can fight for, like 1.5°C for the temperature.

There is no similar number to aim for in terms of biodiversity, which makes it very hard for scientists to install this as part of the story about climate change. We need to be able to measure it.

For example, it could be the size of pathways for hedgehogs through a city. How many centimeters wide should a pathway for hedgehogs be to take them from one point in the city to the other?

Maybe we need a network of biodiversity pathways. If you want to design it you need to give it a substance in terms of space, a dimension.

AB: This reminds me of Edward O. Wilson's Half Earth initiative, a proposal to protect half of the earth's land and oceans in order to preserve biodiversity globally. With this and other initiatives it will be interesting to track how they are implemented, by whom, and who has the capacity to fund it.

RESOURCES

MA: When we were in Luxembourg it was very interesting to see networks and industrial objects down in the forest. In some parts of Luxembourg, there is forest everywhere, but it is nevertheless on the decline.

The question is how to manage forests and who is going to be responsible for them and design them.

AB: Especially because we have such different conditions. Here in a temperate climate, the forest is an unstoppable force. When we stop agriculture or other forms of cultivation, such as gardening or lawn mowing, the forest comes back on its own. You could very quickly transform the south of Luxembourg into a forest if you wanted to. That's not the case in the Mediterranean. It is so much work to plant a tree and keep it alive. And in arid zones, planting a forest would involve a great deal of resources, such as labor, water, fertilizers, and so on.

MA: Over the last few years, we have been referring a great deal to the Balkan condition with urban island systems, zoning regulations with semi-detached houses, and the jungle situation. How to design, increase acceptance of, and manage territories with a jungle aspect is an intriguing question. It was very prevalent at the Venice Biennale last year. In order to make a real impact one approach would be to create a new law, or a kind of urban rule about fallowscapes on a European scale. Our universities focus too much on the construction of buildings and not enough on political science.

PLATFORM

PM: Aglaée said that we are responsible for space. But forests are also responsible for space. They create space through trees but they are also responsible for space. If we want to get through the transition period, we need to collaborate with the other agencies and disciplines that create space. We are not the only ones.

MA: The last three competitions you, Panos, organized are in a way schools or platforms. Maybe not so much inhabitants' platforms but rather research platforms.

PM: Yes, they are designed to be that way. When taught correctly, architects are able—through their interdisciplinary approaches—to also become process designers, creating design objects and territories. Process design is very interesting.

Transition will only become a reality if you prioritize the project itself and let your name disappear in the process. But this is not what our schools are made for.

I want to challenge the idea that architects only design buildings or cities and highlight the fact that they can also design processes. I want to bring about a change of perspective.

If you put an architect, a planner, and a politician together to undertake the project of transition they will all want to have their names on it. That's why it is not going to work. Transition will only become

a reality if you prioritize the project itself and let your name disappear in the process. But this is not what our schools are made for. Our schools create designers, engineers, etc., who want their names to be visible, to be the creator, the person to talk about.

The solution lies more in the links as part of an entire network than in any single link itself.

This platform should be such that at the end the ingredients get mingled to create a new DNA, something new. This is what real interdisciplinarity is about.

During the 19th century, the universities introduced geography, history, sociology, architecture, because these were the problems of their time. They took the name of the problems and they made disciplines out of them. And we are still working with the burden of the 19th century university as we are trying to resolve current questions which are asking us to take everything apart. But we can't because we're working within an old system.

AD: That old system is certainly related to silo thinking. A certain specialization of knowledge is necessary, and this, as Panos says, must be redefined according to the problems to be solved, but above all we need to rethink the relationship between these specializations.

Now, our work follows a competitive approach, but if we can find a collaborative way of working the specializations might be valuable.

The connection between the specialized disciplines needs to be much more based on fluid intelligence than it is now. The solution lies more in the links as part of an entire network than in any single link itself.

Fig. 78: Aglaée Degros

TERRITORY

MA: What is interesting in the complexity and the size of the large-scale territory tasks is teaching the students not to find easy answers with a project but to take time to get lost in scales and disciplines, and then to investigate with obstinacy. It is only then that the role, the position, and the commitment appear.

PM: You're taking the right approach. At the moment there is no protocol to unite different approaches to form a coherent whole.

This would allow the forest that Anita was talking about to come to life.

PLATFORM

PM: Governments are silo systems that repeat the same mistakes as the universities because they are based on tree-like structures that are related to a fossil or pre-fossil fuel era. Whereas today we are taking a big leap forward in understanding the world through scientific discoveries and mathematics, expecting quantum computing to soon come out. What we have been doing for the last 2000 years seems to be totally inappropriate and useless.

AB: We also need less partisanship for true collaboration aimed at the discovery of new concepts, including open debates and discussion with stakeholders not normally included. For example, there is enormous potential to reinvent streets with the introduction of driverless cars. Streets occupy at least 30 percent of the surface of the city, and in the United States cars occupy 50 percent.

Up to now architects have been in alliance with builders, cement industries, high-tech industries, and politicians but much less so with ecologists. There are no ecology courses at architectural schools.

The efficiency this new technology will afford can potentially release a significant amount of space in the street corridor, which opens up the possibility for new paradigms regarding streets of the future. This is clearly an opportunity for introducing more robust urban forestry programs that will mitigate heat islands and absorb CO_2, yet this will work against established practices that prioritize cars. Who decides and who has priority given changing values and emerging paradigms?

AD: That's very interesting. We are in a technological context and the question is always what goal we want to achieve. In the Luxembourg master studio, students tried to optimize space while considering options made possible by digital technology. But yes, Anita, when we optimize we need to question what we are optimizing for.

RR: AI, ICTs, and big data can contribute to optimizing the space. But we need to critically question the fact that the AIs and ICTs are developed primarily by global IT companies in a demand-generating manner. We need a people-centered, integrated, transition-orientated approach towards tech innovations in urban design that goes beyond neoliberal concepts. They must be designed for the common good.

One way could be to design them but you could also plant in a way that the plants themselves will redesign it organically.

AB: We need to focus on adapting to climate change and on making climate adaptation a universal right for all. We need to focus on adapting to climate change and on making climate adaptation a universal right for all.

PM: The point is that we do not have the right lobbies in the right place in law making. All political decisions are realized by laws and regulation. It's a very interesting example you are giving. This means we should be seeking the right alliances. Up to now architects have been in alliance with builders, cement industries, high-tech industries, and politicians but much less so with ecologists. There are no ecology courses at architectural schools.

This means that if we believe in the transition projects, instead of going to the Venice Biennale of Architecture we should be going to Glasgow to see the COP26.

RESOURCES

AD: During the recent conference "on scale" at the USI, the issue of the transformation and naturalization of rivers was discussed. One way could be to design them but you could also plant in a way that the plants themselves will redesign it organically. Not only does this mean that, as with the forest, the plants of the river become an agent of development, but it also means that the design of the river space comes from the way in which the sediments will settle in relation to the plants. The scientific disciplines and design disciplines have to work together on such a transformation.

Our discipline has the ability to foresee the transition—we have the capacity to show what the future of transition could be. We can show better than scientists. They can explain why something is a certain way, but we can show where we are going. This is a great advantage in the transformation of space.

PLATFORM

PM: Aglaée, I agree with that. Our professions have been inventing and organizing inhabitable environments, making them into places where human beings could survive well, thrive, develop, etc.

By definition our clients are humans. As long as we are designing for humans, we design with the tools of today. We need to approach the profession from the perspective of archaeology and sociology to see how and why it exists. Where does your income come from, what is the value chain, who asks you to do something? Is it a private client, a prince, the pope, etc.? If it's a human being that is one thing. But if it's a more-than-human, or a complex client, then this client needs to be able to communicate their needs.

We have to reinvent this cycle of interested parties. We have to reinvent the client. We have to reinvent the way we articulate the mission. We have to reinvent the way we are paid for architectural commissions. We don't know how to do that. But I'm sketching out the process to see who can interact. This is what schools of architecture should reinvent if we want to make the transition a viable project. Anita, do you think it is possible to redesign the whole chain?

AB: We have done some studios like this, but we need to restructure it in a more interdisciplinary way. And I agree with you Aglaée, that we are responsible for space and for the quality of the environment in its ecological and experiential sense because no other discipline can do it. But we also have to be much more comfortable knowing when we design for whom and for what, to reinvent the client and the program as you say, as well as the parameters of a project.

As architects we are used to working on utopian visions, but we should start thinking about dystopian visions.

UNCERTAINTY

PM: I recently read an article exclaiming "Stop Everything Now." This is something which Extinction Rebellion also brings up. It is understandable because there is a need to pause and see what we have done. But it is impossible to stop everything. Instead we should work more with the idea of urgency. We are working in a state of urgency. In Europe we see the consequences of the climate emergency: fire, flood, heat islands, etc.

MA: If we want to truly prioritize ecology we have to dismantle the system. Fallowland, for example, can only be cultivated at a specific time;

by definition, things run at a slower pace and its size and territory are different. But we don't need to stop everything.

RR: Indeed, we are facing the ecological urgency that has been clear since the nineties. Scientists have been raising awareness about that urgency for years, which hasn't changed much although the environmental risks are becoming very obvious.

According to Jem Bendell, we have around ten years to solve the climate crisis and become not only CO_2-neutral, but CO_2-positive in order to be able to capture the CO_2 and reverse current climatic dynamics.

As architects we are used to working on utopian visions, but we should start thinking about dystopian visions.

Fig. 79: Radostina Radulova-Stahmer

VII.

Positions

Many different kinds of agents are needed for the territorial transition. The following eight positions broaden the relational network of the transition, offering different perspectives from environmentalists, landscape architects, philosophers, urbanists, and architects. The positions contribute to a holistic alignment of academia and practice.

The diversity of positions also links aspects such as revolution, ecological value, density, carbon metrics, obsolescence, uncertainty, innovative tools, scale, the transition in practice, resources, or the metabolism in the digital transformation. The positions make it possible to identify valuable connections that invite a further densification of the relational network towards the territorial transition.

Stefan Bendiks
The making of

Eva Schwab
Value-able ecological transition?

Simon Hartmann
Fear of the dark

Marc Armengaud
Who wants to start a revolution?

Florian Dupont
Density and carbon emission

Matthijs Bouw
Toward a new equation

Ingrid Taillandier
Desired density

Radostina Radulova-Stahmer
Territorial metabolism in digital change

Positions

The making of

Stefan Bendiks

What is described, discussed, and illustrated in this book—the transition from territories that have yet to be defined, by the way, to a decarbonization and ecological turnaround—asks for nothing less than what is generally referred to as a paradigm shift. However, this is not in the sense of a scientific revolution for which we have to throw established theories overboard—Einstein's theory of relativity is still valid (as of today) and scientists have known about climate change for decades. The paradigms we need to question and change are more about concrete solutions to problems that the experts have accepted.[1]

So it is not (only) about theory and facts, but about taking action and overcoming habitual ways of acting and approaches to solutions in the face of framework conditions that seem to have suddenly changed. Reacting to profound changes, questioning, and ultimately radically adapting one's own actions is a challenging process. After all, it involves throwing overboard routines and norms that have been in place for decades. This is not an easy undertaking, especially when these seem to have proven themselves in everyday professional life in the past. This is not a problem of a single profession but is cross-disciplinary: the urban planner holds on to the instrument of development plans; the traffic planner to his traffic models. Before the means and answers can be altered, we must first realize that the issues have changed:

Urban planning is no longer just about accommodating real estate investments as well as possible in the city but about questioning whether and where demographic and programmatic shifts (also outside one's own city limits) make the most sense.

Urban planning is no longer just about accommodating real estate investments as well as possible in the city but about questioning whether and where demographic and programmatic shifts (also outside one's own city limits) make the most sense.

And transport planning is no longer just about how to get the most cars into and out of the city without traffic jams, but how to give all people access to suitable mobility options.

1 Kuhn, *The Essential Tension.* Kuhn, *The Structure of Scientific Revolutions.*

Positions

These two disciplines are also explicitly mentioned here because with Artgineering we work at the interface between urban planning and mobility in many of our projects, as well as with more or less cross-border territories. Two examples of larger, longer-term transition processes are the Radoffensive Graz 2030[2] and the *T.OP Noordrand*[3] project described in this book. Both have a time horizon of more than ten years and go beyond political and administrative boundaries.

Also, many of the project owners in the area found the most important subject areas—education and ecology, which we defined together with the stakeholders in workshops—too abstract for them to identify with.

In the territorial development plan for the northern edge of Brussels, the first challenge was that no one, except the project initiators themselves, understood the Noordrand as a territorial entity. Also, many of the project owners in the area found the most important subject areas—education and ecology, which we defined together with the stakeholders in workshops—too abstract for them to identify with.

The topic of mobility offered more concrete starting points in this respect: in order to get the very different private and public actors to work together, we defined axes that were easier to communicate as generally understandable, comprehensible spatial entities. The multimodal "European boulevard" from the Gare du Midi train station to the airport was concrete and concise enough to inspire the different actors and encourage them to work together beyond their own interests. The boulevard as a spatially and mentally connecting construct was in hindsight the best suited to bring together the most diverse actors (public transport providers, hotel chains, airport, city and region, NATO, cycling representatives, etc.) and their interests. It was possible to bring together planned and future projects and to develop synergies. Concrete transport projects that emerged from the European Boulevard scenario are, for example, the extension of a tram line to the airport and the faster implementation of a cycle highway through the area. In addition to working with the spatial entity of the boulevard, which facilitates identification, another important success factor was the starting point of working with actual projects and their owners/initiators. There was no attempt to impose an abstract vision for the northern edge on the local actors but to find and create added value in the context of the various existing initiatives. The

2 "Masterplan Radoffensive Graz 2030"

3 "Territoriaal Ontwikkelings-programma Noordrand"

overarching strategy for the entire territory that ultimately emerged from this was then understood by the participating actors as their own.

The Radoffensive Graz 2030 is a 100-million-Euro program to improve the cycling infrastructure of the Graz conurbation, as part of the larger process of the city's transport transition. The project is set up for a period of at least ten years and includes the city of Graz as well as surrounding municipalities and the province of Styria. The original project approach was mainly traffic-related: the priority was to increase the share of cycling through the construction of appropriate infrastructure. However, it was also foreseeable that a sectoral objective would meet with resistance from other modes of transport, as well as from those in charge of green space and public space. In the master plan, we therefore worked to bring other sectors and administrative levels on board from the beginning. The objectives of the Radoffensive were expanded and formulated in such a way that they not only considered the concerns of cyclists, but also took into account pedestrians and public transport, as well as the improvement of the quality of public space and the question of more green spaces. This created the basis for more open and less sectoral discussions and negotiations with other departments of the city and state, expert planners, and also with the population and businesses.

Good cooperation between the authorities of the city and the state is a particularly important factor here. In many mobility projects that cross the city limits, different political colors (the progressive city usually being surrounded by a more conservative area) and different interests of the population (quality of life in the city versus congestion-free commuting) cause conflicts and ultimately blockades. In Graz, the interplay between city and country has worked surprisingly well so far, despite different political parties in power. The awareness that mobility challenges do not stop at the city limits is present on both sides. What certainly also helps is that cycling is now supported by the majority, even among conservative voters.

What certainly also helps is that cycling is now supported by the majority, even among conservative voters.

However, the example of the Radoffensive in Graz also shows how important it is to have a clear political message in addition to a cross-geographical, cross-sectoral, cross-actor, and cross-administrative approach. Especially in the case of long-term, complex, and transboundary transition processes,

Positions

political leaders are needed who have the courage to point out new paths and demand that the administrations throw out old-established routines and norms.

Clearly, territorial transition is not possible without courageous, proactive politics and a strong, competent public administration.

The issue here is that administrations tend to be rather inflexible in their organization and structure. They are also more or less independent of political agendas—which is, by the way, not necessarily a bad thing in times of populist volatility in politics. To bring about a paradigm shift in the implementation of projects in this context requires a strong impulse and perseverance. Clearly, territorial transition is not possible without courageous, proactive politics, and a strong, competent public administration. That is why we have invested a lot of time and energy in the Radoffensive, not only to convince the political decision-makers of the merits of the project and give them the arguments they need to promote the topic but also in capacity-building of the administration and specialist planners on the topic of cycling and the interdisciplinary cooperation.

Some of the lessons learned from the two projects mentioned here are generally valid for advancing complex and controversial projects: sufficient funding, political will, competent people, and—not yet explicitly mentioned—adequate regulations and legislation. Others are, from our experience, specifically relevant for territorial transition projects:

Starting with existing projects and initiatives and thus also with their project owners and initiators; working towards (unexpected) coalitions of actors in the territory, including the project owners just mentioned; and breaking down the complex territorial contexts into understandable and accessible spatial units.

Of course, this is not a patent remedy for territorial transition. Every territory and every transition task is different, with its own potentials and challenges. Engaging with and responding to both the physical and the non-physical context is crucial.

Positions

Valueable ecological transition?

Eva Schwab

When the roundtable discussion touched upon the necessary metrics to inspire and assess an ecological transition, one dimension was lingering in the background of the conversation—that of economy. So let me start this essay with a question:

How much would you be willing to pay for five more trees on your street?

Many will be hard-pressed for an answer to this topic, and that not only because it begs even more questions as one is busy finding replies to the first.

With this question, we find ourselves at the center of the debate surrounding "ecosystem services," a concept that has gained currency in planning departments around the world as commodification and economization influence our ways of thinking about climate change and loss of biodiversity.

The concept of "ecosystem services" has been put forward to raise awareness of the (economic) value of nature for our society, a value that often remains hidden because the environment's services

are seemingly available free of charge and without limit. It follows from the understanding that well-functioning and diverse nature is the fundamental basis for the economy and people's well-being.

Numerous studies have pointed out this economic dimension and shown that investments in the protection of nature also pay off in macroeconomic terms.

Numerous studies have pointed out this economic dimension and shown that investments in the protection of nature also pay off in macroeconomic terms.

Ecosystem service thinking tries to assess the actual financial value of the many services that nature provides[1] to human society by adding in the costs for health, productivity, and infrastructure if these services were not rendered or if technical solutions would be installed instead; for example when New York City paid farmers more than $1 billion

[1] Services include three main areas: provisioning, such as the production of food and water; regulating, such as the control of climate and disease and upkeep of air, water, and soil quality; and cultural, such as spiritual, educational, and recreational benefits.

Positions

to change their farm management practices to prevent animal waste and fertilizer from washing into the waterways. This saved the city $6–8 billion on a new water filtration plant and $300–500 million of annual running costs. In this way, the idea of ecosystem services aims at providing arguments for political and urban planning decisions, also in participatory planning.

But what if we were to say that our current economic system is unsustainable and only serves to exacerbate existing social and ecological problems?

Such an approach is clearly anthropocentric, asking what nature "does" for us humans and how we can translate these services into easily understandable (economic) metrics.

But what if we were to say that our current economic system is unsustainable and only serves to exacerbate existing social and ecological problems?[2]

What if the environment was understood not only as a neutral resource or as a provider of services but as having an intrinsic value? What if we tried to understand human settlement not only as serving the needs of humans, as not only shaped by human activity, but as complex, hybrid, networked settlement space which is "more-than-human," and in

which particularly the co-existence and co-dependence of humans and non-humans needs to be highlighted?[3]

This would then fundamentally question how our society works in terms of economy.

As immense social and ecological crises[4] reveal themselves in different forms all over the world, it becomes increasingly clear that the building sector plays an important role in this. To meet our climate goal, the industry not only needs to decarbonize, it also needs to become regenerative. In light of this, it is more than legitimate to erase the if from the aforementioned questions and acknowledge that today's main economic paradigm—that of GDP growth—is unable to solve the current challenges in our rich, democratic, European context, especially as we know that economic growth in the past was twinned with increasing greenhouse gas emissions.

Critical research over the last years has highlighted how "green growth" and "sustainable development" evolved into a market logic that goes hand in hand with a "pluralization" of the state. This means that governance is shared between political representatives, experts, and private actors engaged in the delivery and financing of so-called sustainable and smart cities. It, moreover, has led to empowering business elites, negating issues of democracy and

2 Kate Raworth argues: "Attempting to sustain GDP growth in an economy that may actually be close to maturing can drive governments to take desperate and destructive measures. [...] They add the living world into the national accounts as 'ecosystem services' and 'natural capital,' assigning it a value that looks dangerously like a price." In: Raworth: *Doughnut Economy*, 296.

3 Non-human refers to both the natural world and artificial intelligence.

4 For example, climate change, ocean acidification, loss of biodiversity, or challenges such as poverty, lack of education, and shortage of affordable housing, which observed together give reason to question the existence of social solidarity on both a local and global level.

accountability as well as "naturalizing the political" in a way that failed to find new, more equitable and environmentally sound ways of handling our necessary ecological transition.

There is, however, at the same time "a new wave of activism that struggles to bring the environmental question back into the heart of public concern. These struggles link environmental justice to social justice."

This raises a number of (perhaps uncomfortable) professional questions. To list only a few: How can architects and planners position themselves vis-a-vis this situation? How can they devise ways of working that foster distributive and regenerative approaches, especially knowing that "[s]ystemic change happens at a snail's pace because vested interests and lobby groups rule. [...] The construction industry is enormously corrupted by vested interests."[5] How, then, can planners' and designers' honorarium be decoupled from construction, in the light of the fact that new builds will need to be the exception (in Europe and other rich regions of the world) if we are to stand a chance against the looming climate catastrophe?

Ways to promote human prosperity (and not economic growth) through a regenerative and distributive environment are already in the air. Possible solutions include circular material use and systems of buildings that have rooftops for the production of food, that generate energy, sequester carbon dioxide, clean the air, treat their own wastewater, and turn sewage back into rich soil nutrients. They also include sponge cities to absorb excess water as well as vegetation to improve the microclimate and biodiversity corridors. They encompass improved models for land value capture, municipalities which are willing to negotiate private developments and set quality standards benefitting the collective, and robust spatial structures that are open to housing shared facilities and giving room to a sharing economy.

Above all, they include the understanding that the imaginary separation of humans from nature (also expressed in city vs. nature or rural vs. urban thinking) is counterproductive when we need to find systemic ways of working which are distributive and regenerative by design.

5 Original: "Systemische Veränderungen passieren im Schneckentempo, weil Besitzstandswahrer und Lobbygruppen walten. Aber auch in weniger stark regulierten Ländern ist es kompliziert, weil wirtschaftliche Interessen dominieren. Die Bauwirtschaft ist von den eigenen Interessen enorm korrumpiert"

Positions

Fear of the dark

Simon Hartmann

"Fear Of The Dark" refers to the masterful song on the eponymous 1992 album by Iron Maiden, the British heavy metal band around bass player and leading composer Steve Harris. One of the striking things about heavy metal is that the personal perspective of a song text often triggers crowds of 50,000 people to slip into a trance-like state.

But whether this is true or not, the song manages to embrace something unpleasant we all have to deal with sometimes and to lift it to a hymn with the opposite effect of its literal content.

Evil fantasies, nightmares, or in this case, the "fear of the dark" become a collective moment of joy. Steve Harris, who wrote the song, is said to suffer from nyctophobia, a fear of darkness. But whether this is true or not, the song manages to embrace something unpleasant we all have to deal with sometimes and to lift it to a hymn with the opposite effect of its literal content.

1 Vogt, "Étienne-Louis Boullée visits the Tate Modern."

Resource before authorship:

In 2003, Adolf Max Vogt raises the provocative question of who to credit for the Tate Modern's architecture.[1] He supports the idea that the decisive factor for the result is the building type rather than the authorship of an architect. According to Vogt, the sublime dimensions of the turbine hall within the power station designed by architect Sir Giles Gilbert Scott were necessary to fulfill a building task. "Scott had no other choice." Vogt credits "the later discoverer of the station in its ruined state, Tate Gallery director Sir Nicholas Serota" and Herzog & de Meuron with arriving "at a renewed refreshing whole that never withholds a certain respect for the old building by Scott" while avoiding the cliché of the conventional museum because they "insist on claiming a suitable portion of the work for their own art." This list of Tate Modern authors is undoubtedly still a woodcut-like simplification of reality. Still, I think it represents a beautiful and contemporary view of authorship because it puts the building before the author.

Positions

Carambole and the anticipation of future uncertainty:

Urs Füssler, a Berlin-based architect with Swiss origins, put forward an interesting thought in Das Carambole-Prinzip. The text is the transcript of a lecture conceived as a commented journey through Berlin. The very personal starting point is how a young Swiss who grew up in the Jurassic mountains discovered Berlin in 1981 and speculated on the reasons for specific spatial configurations and architecture he encountered during that walk. Based on his systematic reading of the city, Urs Füssler (2003)[2] developed a design principle called the "principle of carambole." According to this understanding, an architectural intervention should be considered as a strike in carambole billards, where players try to strike two balls consecutively with a third one. Carambole is not about getting rid of the balls but about being able to continue for as long as possible. Therefore it is all about constellations, and the end of each strike is about creating a favorable constellation for the next. The architectural "principle of carambole" asks architects to consider each project from the point of view of how useful it will be as a starting point for the next strike.

Logic of the frugal–reinventing buildings fallen out of use:

In the 1970s, the Yugoslav state entrusted the then young Slovenian architect Marko Mušič (*1944) with the project of a 22,000 square meter building with a wild programmatic mix ranging from a memorial for mothers to a theater for 1000 spectators to a radio and tv station, a disco, exhibition, and convention spaces.

Carambole is not about getting rid of the balls but about being able to continue for as long as possible. Therefore it is all about constellations, and the end of each strike is about creating a favorable constellation for the next.

A jury of about sixty developed the wide-ranging program given to the architect Marko Mušič, who, to quote Adolf Max Vogt, had "no other choice" than to design spaces with sublime dimensions. Dom Revolucije aspired to be an infrastructure for the improvement of cultural life. The architectural decisions taken by Mušič were bold and challenged the possibilities of contemporary construction. President Tito's death and the subsequent falling apart of Yugoslavia prevented the building from ever being finished according

2 Füssler, "Das Carambole-Prinzip."

to the plans and used. What was intended to be the catalyst of and the symbol for progress and growth of the small, provincial, and very industrial town of Nikšić turned out to be a burden inherited from the socialist past and the main symbol of a society in decline.

When looking at it from the perspective of the principle of carambole, the unfinished Dom Revolucije was a constellation no one was able to play.

When looking at it from the perspective of the principle of carambole, the unfinished Dom Revolucije was a constellation no one was able to play.

A landscape free from architectural authorship and contemporary cultural intentions but with the potential to become an exciting new place for human activities within a framework oscillating between building and nature.

In 2018 we, HHF, and our colleagues, architects Sadar+Vuga from Slovenia, teamed up for the international architecture competition organized to deal with the ruinous landscape of Dom Revolucije. And we won by turning around the question by asking how

3 Kosec, "An Architectural Jam Session."

new uses can adapt to what was there rather than converting or adjusting the building. We read the existing condition of Dom Revolucije as a landscape rather than a building. A landscape free from architectural authorship and contemporary cultural intentions but with the potential to become an exciting new place for human activities within a framework oscillating between building and nature.

Process-oriented collectivism:

During the project's development, we reached out to the young Slovenian architecture theorist Miloš Kosec, who wrote and described our design process as a jam session involving past and future protagonists instead of a performance.[3] He describes non-use as a collaborative process that invites you to be part of something. From that perspective, becoming a ruin should not be seen as problematic or even wrong in architecture but as something genuinely positive, a process of opening up for something new. Decay is the most recent layer of information one can read on a building and society. What do we let go of? What do we leave behind and what do we maintain? And what about the question of scale, as a building too big, almost geographical. We find deltas, erosions, tectonic movements, but also an economic question: a resource space that it would be impossible to entirely control. The power of the monument defines its territory of origin and yet the specific issues of this object in this city and its state can make it a lesson of transition. Using some of the remaining infrastructure, waiting, recognizing the potentials, content with the minimum of action to reorient everything. This is a landscape that resulted partly from the unfinished architectural project and partly from natural processes fostered by the neglect of the Post-Yugoslav society.

Our aim was to breathe life into a stillborn architecture altered and partly taken over by nature. Sadly, we could not continue our strikes and create the hymn intended to celebrate those same spaces that inflict fear today. Our successful first strikes made other parties believe in their capacities to take over the game of carambole, and they did so without hesitation. A wrecking company was brought in during a weekend by a powerful local politician who ordered them to remove all building parts reminiscent of the political and social ambition of Dom Revolucije. The architectural and programmatic banality of what was since built might be qualified as alive. Still, it is not Dom Revolucije, but the zombie version using some of the original body parts.

Positions

Who wants to start a revolution?
Note on the profession of transition planner.
Marc Armengaud

How far should planners and architects drift to the vanguard?

Efforts to plan the ecological transition have generated a string of international competitions that tend to put architects and planners in

> Efforts to plan the ecological transition have generated a string of international competitions that tend to put architects and planners in awkward and possibly untenable political positions.

awkward and possibly untenable political positions, as they are asked to accomplish radical transformations under the guise of design projects that will have political impacts far beyond the architect's mandate. Specific technical requests (zero net emissions, local scale management of resources, etc.), reflect hyperbolic political goals: rethink energy, rethink water, rethink food, rethink the forest, the countryside, transport, logistics, networks, and by the way, rethink health too… While this is a remarkable moment for architects, tackling such issues will translate into difficult changes with mandatory consequences for businesses, corporations, administrations and private citizens alike, a lot of which might be painful and destabilizing. After decades of criticism against the violence of Modernism and its social and environmental consequences, development projects are now expected to break away from standard practices in order to confront an extraordinary state of emergency. As politicians only expect development projects to adopt a set of revised norms, the ideological demand actually comes from the public servants and consultants who write these ground-shaking briefs. Dedicated to the transformational vision of the "transition," these technicians are formulating new equations, dimensioned from the latest scientific reports, which are never really publicly debated, possibly because voters would be scared off. Architects end up having to sort out major political questions, the practical details of which neither politicians nor voters want to hear about.

Transition—transgression

In the context of biennales and academic lectures, architects love to debate the Anthropocene. But are they ready or even able to design and implement projects that take up the magnitude of the task? The ecological transition calls for transgressions that remain largely unthought or silent: each architect needs to make their own leap of faith! Is this a pre-revolutionary situation? In theoretical terms, the ongoing radical change of perspective is a Copernican revolution which affects projects as well. In political terms, fundamental shifts in the organization and management of societies seem unavoidable, which eventually might overthrow the current status quo of powers and interests. And in terms of cultural transformations, the ecological transition is already present as a social revolution

combining the counter-cultural spirit of the late 1960s with darker tones from the 1990s cyberpunk era. In this context, there is a risk that transition plans may remain stuck in a neutral sphere that would remain cosmetic at best, or at worst be resented as the political tool of technocratic authoritarianism. Is it then up to architects to plan and design new forms of governance, in order to support the transition's goals?

Where are the Bastille walls?

How relevant is the idea of revolution anyway? The return of Marxist theory in recent years has brought back familiar 19th century political constructions, defined by fronta conflicts and dialectic struggles.

The Ecological Transition calls for transgressions that remain largely unthought or silent: to each architect their own leap of faith! Is this a pre-revolutionary situation?

But are we really living a reality structured by frontal oppositions anymore? Complexity at the global scale and the multitude of local fights for identity and survival are anything but frontal, and capitalism is a very elusive adversary. There are no walls to besiege, there is no central entity to decapitate! Should we place our hopes in the climatic stress as a generator of collective unanimity, or should we be ready to act within fragmented or at least very differentiated social configurations and deal with that?

Should we place our hopes in the climatic stress as a generator of collective unanimity, or should we be ready to act within fragmented or at least very differentiated social configurations and get along with that?

The conversation between theory and governance is already happening within hybrid frameworks such as those developed by Bruno Latour (or inspired by him), a sociologist who has moved beyond the constraints of disciplines in order to enter the field of action. The "Parlement de la Loire[1]" has become a role model for non-governmental institutions, able to reframe a vast body of issues and resources and force the political stakeholders to participate and provide answers. Such non-frontal experiments are definitely projects, although not developed under the authority of designing architects. In this case, national and local institutions tried to get on board with the AMITER competitions.[2] Everything worked well as long as the French

Ministry of Sustainable Development directed the process. But when juries convened, the local politicians didn't understand what it was about, and rejected the proposals that advocated for accepting floods as a driving force for planning, which was actually the competition's baseline goal! The revolution will not follow a straight line...

Off-screen guerilla

It is remarkable that in the last decade, academic and cultural institutions, as well as grassroots organizations, have launched consultations that have not been located within the framework of standard administrations, making it possible for more progressive and experimental stances to be expressed and debated, with direct impact on the way later projects have been implemented. Innovation is always reclaimed by the centralizing institutions, but most of the time appears away from the mainstream. Off-screen means here: not necessarily in the framework of a world scale metropolis, and not necessarily under the lead of professional planners and public commissioners.

In the Main-Rhein Region around Frankfurt, Wiesbaden, and Mainz, a local non-profit organization bringing together planners, architects, academics, and artists teamed up with the DAM (Deutsches Architektur Museum). Together they have been

1 "Démarche du parlement de Loire."

2 "Concours AMITER."

running several international work-shops with forward thinking European planning and design offices, aiming to rethink their region in sustainable terms. The Main-Rhein area is one of the EU's most impressive economic powerhouses, but it is also a polluted post-industrial territory paralyzed by internal competition between rival political structures (different cities and different Länder). The resulting debates, exhibitions, and publications[3] encouraged challenging questions and provocative solu-tions, precisely because they were conducted differently, and targeted the wider public as well as develop-ment professionals and politicians.

Another example could be the initiative of the Luma Foundation in Arles, a contemporary art institution which also acts as an informal terri-torial incubator for the entire Rhône Delta region. Luma brings together an impressive variety of relevant territorial agents within the formats of yearly events (Luma days)[4] where grassroots development strategies are collectively debated. The delta is possibly the richest agricultural area in Europe, but it is now facing the inescapable prospect of sea-rise, drought, and flooding, without the support of any heavy-weight polit-ical capital. Luma has its roots in a private natural protection area set up in Camargue in the early 1950s, and has the credibility to gather farmers, architects, hotel managers,

chefs, and artists in order to start up practical and cultural collaborations, moving towards a future that cannot be defined by a frontal fight against a single threat: instead there is a set of attitudes that make sense in order to confront and retain some form of control over the many revolutions that will happen simultaneously.

How do you fight a monster that is the result of all your mistakes (often thought of as achievements)? Correcting past mistakes won't be enough, and often impossible.

Trying the un-tempered piano to tame Godzilla...

The complex entanglement of negative conditions that we need to confront now and in the next decades is monstrous. So how do you fight a monster that is the result of all your mistakes (often thought of as achievements)? Correcting past mistakes won't be enough, and often impossible. And envisioning the future is extremely difficult because of the chaotic nature of the climate's disruptions. Transgressions in meth-odology, technology, and manage-ment are easier to innovate where there is a lack of overarching gover-nance, and non-standard players

3 See: Living the Region, directed by Kaï Vöckler, Felix Nowak and Christian Holl, DAM, Warmth Verlag, Berlin 2018.

4 See: Luma Days, https://www.luma.org/fr/arles/nous-connaitre/les-projets/Luma-Days.html

must step in to fill in. Such off-screen configurations are very diverse: the countryside is an obvious one, but night-time[5] is a surprising parallel state of reality. Technical systems, such as networks, also tend to run in parallel realities (underground, hidden, and far away) and provide strong leverage for transition. Shifting our attention to fringe, lateral, and non-standard situations is a strategic path for making breakthrough statements and undertaking novel experiments that have the ability to affect the more conventional practices and accelerate their cultural, political, and technical transition. After centuries of functionalist rationalism that dealt with each problem in separate boxes, the monster that we have to deal with is fundamentally chaotic: unpredictable and violent. Our relationship to the future cannot be linear and precise anymore. So what are projects supposed to do? Well, they need to provide new tools made to measure for the transition, but also provide a stage for the many revolutions to be tested, big or small...

[5] See: Publications by AWP, Paris la Nuit, Chroniques nocturnes, and Pavillon de l'Arsenal. 2013, Nightscapes, GG, 2009.

Positions

Density and carbon emission

Florian Dupont

Carbon will become a central unit of measurement over the coming years. You're probably realizing that you don't know exactly what this unit refers to—well, carbon is basically a way of measuring energy transfers. Almost all energy processes release greenhouse gases into the atmosphere which increases global warming. And every year we fail to reduce these emissions, carbon becomes more important as the decisive factor in all aspects of life. Therefore, in your lifetime, you will see this constraint becoming more and more important, maybe up to a point where it will be as important as money.

In our practice, we work on quite ambitious competitions from a carbon perspective where the ton of carbon per square meter is more important in the decision-making process than the price per square meter.

I want to share how we start our argument when approaching most of our jobs. The first step is looking at large figures. The precise numbers are not that important because there are different ways of counting. What is important is the scale. Basically, in order to reduce the carbon footprint of Europeans by five by 2050 we need to induce and accept massive changes.

And every year we fail to reduce these emissions, carbon becomes more important as the decisive factor in all aspects of life.

We're speaking of changing everything about our lifestyle: the way we move, consume, eat, inhabit, work, etc. This will create a very different life, and we don't yet know what form it will take! In planning you always start by looking at mobility. The carbon impact of mobility must be reduced to a third of what it is now. That's a huge step to take and means that you not only need to change the type of mobility used, but you have to move less. And that's something really important that you have to bear in mind when you're undertaking urban design. All the calculations that we're doing on projects right now show that workplaces are too far away from homes. And even though people are trying to choose their dwellings based on accessibility, and even if it's public transport, it doesn't solve the problem because there's always another family member who isn't capable of going by foot, by bike, or by public transportation. I believe this situation will change the way we see real estate, because we want to have more and more uses in these buildings.

There is no being too ambitious when it comes to carbon reduction and therefore you always have to push radical changes forward.

Mixed use buildings are becoming more and more frequent in urban projects, but we probably haven't reached the point where it allows the level of demobility required while reducing the need of square meters.

In the work we're doing with AWP, we try to see what an alternative design of 10% of our project could do for the city and try to integrate activities that don't exist locally to avoid transportation. For example, 20 hectares of permaculture could provide enough fruits and vegetables for 10,000 people. This changes the way you consume, reducing your

carbon footprint while also providing access to nature and space for biodiversity to flourish.

One main idea that I use all the time is: be radical. We need to understand that being radical now is very different from ten years ago because many politicians and executives now understand the radicality of the carbon equation. So, there is some kind of consensus around radicality. There is no being too ambitious when it comes to carbon reduction and therefore you always have to push radical changes forward.

The second idea to consider is that there is no consensus in the sense that everybody says, well, we have to reduce carbon emissions by five or six and, furthermore, nobody knows what that society will look like. So there is a need for debate on how we can all achieve this goal, and we need to understand that it's research that we will do as a generation. In projects, if politicians do not share the radicality and are not aiming for the same type of carbon neutral society, there is no hope for a consensus.

The third idea involves focusing on how we deal with the current situation. As touched on earlier, the current generation will be much more about refurbishing and trying to bring about change to that which already exists in the city. In this context, you need to think of every project as an opportunity to redirect society toward carbon education.

So how do you do all that? Well, there are two aspects of dealing with this idea of transition that I would like to share here.

The first one is imperfection. Why is it important? It's important because none of your projects will reach their goals straight away. So we are going to fail for the next 10 years, maybe 20 years. If we take all of these setbacks as a global failure, we won't be able to progress and we won't be able to move together in the direction of the energy transition. We need to adopt a particular collective approach to dealing with the issues. It will take time to find the right path and we don't yet know what it will look like. So we need to accept imperfections as part of a path toward our goal. This needs to become integral to the way we work on projects because at the moment there are many things in the field that are not happening because there's always one individual in the room saying, "Well, that doesn't work," or "I'm not doing it because they're not doing it." You hear this all the time. So something we really need to understand is that all our everyday experiences and routines will be challenged again and again. This makes imperfection a central element.

The second important aspect is sourcing. We're living in a time when we're trying to innovate while at the same time making all these innovations suitable for the masses. This is something we need to do with the people that bring about this innovation and with those who are going to use it. And that can only work if you go to these people, and understand what they can do and what they cannot do.

So we need to accept imperfections as part of a path toward our goal.

We will reach a point where everything needs to change; we need to bring all these people together and get them to understand each other. This enables us to move fast, because this transition is about being quick.[1]

[1] Selected pieces from the conference at École nationale supérieure d'architecture de Versailles.

Positions

Toward a new equation

Matthijs Bouw

We see that climate change is accelerating and that assets built today will be confronted with a different climate reality in their useful lifespan. Climate change manifests itself in extreme weather events such as heat, drought, extreme rain, and riverine and coastal flooding.

If spatial development does not take into account the mitigation of these impacts, the shocks and stresses will not only harm the people living there and lead to institutional financial risks but will also cause higher reinvestment costs for climate adaptive measures later on.

If spatial development does not take into account the mitigation of these impacts, the shocks and stresses will not only harm the people living there and lead to institutional financial risks but will also cause higher reinvestment costs for climate adaptive measures later on. What interventions can we implement starting now to build climate resilience and create the foundation for long-term sustainability?

How can we measure our success?

The sustainable transition demands intervention in the systems and networks that connect us. How can we use the next years to ensure we meet our sustainable transition goals?

IPCC's Fifth Assessment Report states that climate change will increase the likelihood of severe, pervasive, and irreversible impacts on people and ecosystems, amplifying existing risks and creating new risks for both.

Now we need to use any opportunity to activate change. One way would be to build knowledge and learn about the capacity for systems change and the efficacy of interventions and actors in reducing Luxembourg's carbon footprint. Or by capacity building by increasing awareness of the necessity for change, the tools and methods to achieve the sustainable transition, and grow the community of citizens, organizations, and institutions who can lead this work through education and involvement. Both, knowledge and capacity building are essential to create meaningful long-term transformation.

The transition requires working from top to bottom, bottom to top, and from visible to invisible, unearthing embedded energy and rethinking demand across multiple systems. We have the technologies for decarbonization. The real question is how to implement it, and how to make sure our investments in decarbonization lead to a better world in general. This is critical because it also provides a feedback loop.

Showing positive results facilitates implementation: institutionally, politically and in the uptake of new technologies by the public. The methodology could start with framing transformations within the individual networks in relation to other networks, by connecting them in territory and space. Associated metrics will help us understand not only the efficacy of the transformations in terms of circularity and resilience, but also their (urban) impacts and implementation pathways.

A second step is to use these territorial and spatial connections as a basis for the formulation of pilot projects.

These pilot projects will provide useful lessons about the suitability of particular interventions for replication and scaling toward 2050. Metrics here will help us understand what works, and what doesn't, and what are barriers and enablers for implementation.

The transition requires working from top to bottom, bottom to top, and from visible to invisible, unearthing embedded energy and rethinking demand across multiple systems.

What are our tools?

The development of scenarios shows that investing more now in a climate robust ecosystem reduces the costs of adaptation for future generations while providing biodiversity and livability co-benefits early. One possible position of experimentation is using pilot projects, which allow us to learn about how to make the first step, the opportunities and challenges for the transition, and to build capacity. The pilot sites can have temporary uses: growing cattail as a building material, clay ripening, energy production, and nitrogen reduction. In these projects, time is seen as a resource for value creation, for now, for when the development is completed, and for future generations. These territorial incubators will form a laboratory for the sustainable transition, as they make it possible to not only dedicate a percentage of infrastructure investments for integration in nearby territories, or to implement a percent fallow land policy to create space for experimentation but also to design, realize, and evaluate pilot projects that will inform the plan for long-term transformation.

In addition, the pilot site can be used to design a process to test opportunities and challenges for each network and thereby allow us to confirm targets and metrics; to develop feasible pilot intervention designs; to align with political and financial considerations; to develop business cases; to implement the pilot project; and to reflect on and learn about the applicability of these interventions for replication and upscaling.

We have to establish metrics now to measure the success of systems interventions according to several attributes. One example is the capacity that describes the ability of actors involved to understand, adapt, and implement. Or one other example is the efficacy which describes risk reduction, carbon reduction, resource use reduction, measurement, and monitoring. But we also need to measure the success of our spatial impact, investing in new locations and creating new ecosystem services; or in terms of social benefit, enabling

improvements to public health, adapting to new ways of life, community participation, and outreach. And last but not least we need to measure our system interventions in terms of cultural and educational added value that impact on public discourse, social and institutional buy-in, and uptake.

Ultimately this is about allowing us to accelerate the process with a new roadmap for the sustainable transition. Through the pilots, we can learn what has the highest chance of success to answer the question of where we should invest, and what are the metrics with which we evaluate (e.g., effectiveness, capacity for scaling and replicating, institutional embedding, etc.).

In conclusion, time supports pre-developing climate adaptive measures in such a way that the urban or any other development can grow into a resilient city now and in the future. Taking also long-term climate impacts into account in the development framework accommodates possibilities for achieving a wider range of residential, economical, and recreational environments that are beneficial both from a climate impact reduction perspective, allowing for less financial risks, and from the perspective of increased livability.[1]

[1] Text issued from the proposition LUX LIT toward a new equation by AWP Office for territorial reconfiguration (Paris) in association with ONE architecture (Matthijs Bouw – risk managment master/ PENN U) – Dirk Sijmons (TU DELFT) – Anita Berrizbeitia (HARVARD GSD) – Aglaée Degros (Graz University of Technology) – Ingrid Taillandier (ITAR) – ARCADIS

Positions

Desired density

Ingrid Taillandier

Ironically, density is a matter of ecology since it militates for mutualization of resources, services, and infrastructures; it is a move towards a frugal approach to economy and land. Beyond the imperative represented by the need for housing, it is nevertheless fundamental to manipulate it according to each territory, based on what is "acceptable" here and without attaching any model to it.

For many, "densify" is an injunction considered in purely quantitative terms, a question of metrics such as people per square kilometer, site coverage, or floor area. However, density is actually a much larger issue that encompasses many other aspects: What is perceived density, built density, or even density? Is density a tool, a prerequisite, or an objective? And what if it were all these things: a way of understanding and responding to environmental challenges, urban sprawl, population growth, and social and demographic problems? We continually take up the immense but exciting challenge of specifying the balances of tomorrow: between density and breathing; between architecture and nature; between individual freedom and a sense of social connection.

Constituted city or new territory; landmark project or dotted line, architecture always obeys the logic of a territory and its history. It sutures, connects, repairs, prolongs, perpetuates, keeps alive or enriches a fabric.

Beyond the imperative represented by the need for housing, it is nevertheless fundamental to manipulate it according to each territory, based on what is "acceptable" here and without attaching any model to it.

Its conception is a matter of negotiation between the different built areas without however neglecting the voids. Sometimes residual but always necessary, the void, this figure of the in-between, is a tool to appropriate uses, define an enviable neighborhood and organize morphological, typological, social, and generational mixes. Whether anthropized or natural, landscape is a common good and an ordinary heritage that construction strives to preserve and reinforce. It is essential to create a framework conducive to

Positions

the establishment of a diversified relationship to nature in order to raise awareness of the challenge and to bring about a sense of peace in everyday life.

How can students explore new ideas about city building to call for more radical thinking in the face of an environmental crisis? To meet the colossal demographic and ecological challenges, how can they question the idea of utopia?

Often decried and always stigmatized, if density has bad press, it is first because of a painful collective memory (at least in France) and a matter of semantics. It is opposed to the suburban model, its harmful psychological role in confinement is pointed out, and it is blamed for social disorder. However, its control reveals variable intensities rather than a dogmatic vision of dense life. Manipulating forms of densities capable of attenuating current crises and going with transitions is the aim of "ecological urbanism"[1] today. Why? Because the challenge for tomorrow's architects and urban planners will lie less in planning than in recovering urban and landscape ecosystems; in understanding and anticipating natural phenomena in which the city and nature can help each other within

1 The Ecole Nationale Supérieure d'architecture de Versailles International Master program is oriented towards "Ecological Urbanism." It is the result of a collaboration with the department of urbanism at Tongji University in Shangai spanning more than 15 years. Many workshops and student exchanges have been organized in this framework. The double master's degree created in 2014 was a new step in the collaboration between our two institutions. It is now extended to other schools' exchange programs.

resilient and innovative habitats; in managing a tool for reclamation of valuable soil.

As practitioners and professors, our main goals and responsibilities are to provide answers to these questions: How can students explore new ideas about city building to call for more radical thinking in the face of an environmental crisis? To meet the colossal demographic and ecological challenges, how can they question the idea of utopia? How can we teach new ways to design cities not disconnected from their environment, finding new links between context and ideology? Today's challenges bear the opportunity for students to become actors and to bring environmental issues to light to re-examine their practice in urban design. In addition to traditional urban analysis tools—planning, socio-economic aspects, spatial zoning, etc.—students learn how to use other tools like risks, metabolism, and bio-dynamism.

Water, energy, time, resources, existing networks, biodiversity, green infrastructure, and geographical dynamics form another dimension of urban thinking.

Intending to identify some obvious or more hidden relationships between contemporary and historical cities, we applied an analytical methodology to a broad range of examples. Through the production and comparison of urban plans and data, we identified similarities in form, as well as various ideological and theoretical underpinnings marking cities' relationship with nature and local resources.

"New cities" was the first topic and prism. Throughout history, they were answers to people's dreams and fears. Their historical form embodied the goals of building a better place for human beings to live, meaning that they could provide key approaches for addressing contemporary situations. Then we studied water cities.

We believe that they have two faces, dealing with water as both a resource and risk: as a natural element to preserve and emphasize, and as a cause of damages that need to be prevented. All the opportunities as well as the threats such as water scarcity, floods, and climate change led to technical, urban, and architectural answers worked on by the students. Today we discuss the topic of density. The case studies focus on recent examples of density in Île de France: the region of Paris and its suburbs. Interviews with actors involved in the construction of neighborhoods, elected officials, developers, urban and landscape planners, and architects help to recall the role of each and to understand the different points of view on density. Density being an extremely subjective notion, surveys with the inhabitants allow us to understand the levers of

well-being that we can use to make density accepted. Going beyond the archetypal approach to density is the first step in acting on the identity of territories, their transitions, and their capacity to accompany demographic movements and changes.

Water, energy, time, resources, existing networks, biodiversity, green infrastructure, and geographical dynamics form another dimension of urban thinking.

Finally, and seemingly paradoxically, these cities and themes analyzed can teach us that facing these serious issues is not only a necessity brought about by an emergency but also the matrix of a certain way of life in which pleasure is consubstantial of responsibilities.

Positions

Territorial metabolism in digital change

Radostina Radulova-Stahmer

The Glasgow Climate Pact parties decided to "emphasizes the importance of strengthening cooperative action on technology development and transfer for the implementation of mitigation and adaptation action [...]".[1] The decisions tackle the technological development in a large number and in a wide range of fields of action.

In order to approach this question, we need to reframe our disciplinary perspective and the logic of the technosphere, consumption, and territorial resources.

We know that technology alone cannot be the solution but what role do the digital transformation and climate tech play for urbanism in addressing the urgent environmental crisis?

We very much need to reflect on the relationship between climate urgency, collective territory, and our task as architects to harness the potential of territorial regenerative capacity in the context of digital transformation. In order to approach this question, we need to reframe our disciplinary perspective and the logic of the technosphere, consumption, and territorial resources. We also need to reformulate the principles and goals of any regenerative design action.

Our collective contribution as humans to global warming has resulted in a significant climate crisis and is putting the planetary boundaries under strain.

Our globalized import-oriented economy is heavily dependent on geopolitical forces and relies on soil capacities all over the globe to meet Western expectations of consumption. The global logistics involved are

[1] United Nation. 2022. Glasgow Climate Pact – Decision -/CP.26.

impacting our ecological footprint and, moreover, increasingly putting into question the opportunities for future human life on the planet. CO_2 emissions are declining far too slowly, reminding us that our discipline is a main contributor to carbon pollution, as the construction sector is responsible for a large portion of global emissions (including mobility-related emissions in the construction sector). For example, the Climate Protection Act stipulates that Germany must be carbon neutral by 2045.

Last year, for example, CO_2 emissions in the transport sector were three million tons above target and in the buildings sector two million tons above target.[2] It is our discipline that is largely responsible for these two areas—urban planning and mobility. Each year, binding targets are set with specific emission limits for energy, buildings, transport, agriculture, industry, and waste management, but unfortunately they are also repeatedly exceeded. So, we need to look at possible spatial-structural approaches to reversing carbon emissions and, if necessary, create artificial carbon sinks, as nature's CO_2 stores are very vulnerable.

At the same time, digital transformation is changing the forms, spaces, and habitats of human and non-human life. Humans have become a geological force in our planet's system. Paul Crutzen described the Anthropocene as a geological age back in 2002, pointing to a global increase in man-made metabolic processes.[3]

Each year, binding targets are set with specific emission limits for energy, buildings, transport, agriculture, industry, and waste management, but unfortunately they are also repeatedly exceeded.

The technosphere includes the realm of technology, machines, factories, computers, cars, buildings, and any mobility infrastructure, to name a few examples.[4] It is considered the "defining system of the Anthropocene,"[5] as a variety of materials taken from the environment are used for the technosphere. Its total mass is 30 billion tons. This already equates to 50 kilograms per square meter today and is five times heavier than the biomass on the planet.[6]

The Global Footprint Network is an international NGO and think tank that measures the ecological footprint to enable informed policy decisions. It describes the necessity of a territorial metabolism because the "ecological overshoot"—the conversion of renewable resources into waste—happens much faster than this waste can be

2 Pinzler, and Schieritz: "Die Politik Der Heißen Luft."

3 Crutzen: "The 'Anthropocene'", 27–32.

4 Mauelshagen: "Technosphere."

5 Haff: "Being Human in the Anthropocene."

6 Zalasiewicz, Waters, Summerhayes, Wolfe, Barnosky, Cearreta, Paul Crutzen, et al. "The Working Group on the Anthropocene: Summary of Evidence and Interim Recommendations."

Positions

converted back into resources. This is because, in contrast to the ecological metabolism in the Anthropocene, we (with our western lifestyles) are responsible for unhealthy linear material flows and wastes that cannot be recycled. This waste will remain on Earth for billions of years, leaving its mark on humanity not only in deep space but also in deep time.

So, we need to look at possible spatial-structural approaches to reversing carbon emissions and, if necessary, create artificial carbon sinks, as nature's CO^2 stores are very vulnerable.

Therefore, we must face the challenge not only to question our understanding of economic growth, of production and consumption, but also to relate it to the anthropocentric urge for territorial ecology. We must take care to design a regenerative industrial metabolism that aims at a circular economy and that is inherently connected to the digital transformation and the technosphere.[7]

With our discipline, we are responsible for designing the supra-regional spatial systems in a way that balances environmental impacts and resource inputs with the territorial capacity to metabolize and regenerate.

Specifically, this could mean creating energy-efficient, low-footprint technologies for resource-optimized reorganization of spatial systems. Or this could mean increasing the available biocapacity[8] by optimizing bioproductivity through a purpose-driven technological deployment to be able to increase the yields of productive ecosystems. What is important here is to avoid possible rebound effects, for example, to avoid negative consequences for biodiversity, or to ensure that the resources used to gain biocapacity do not in turn damage the footprint.[9] Because it is not enough to limit our technological awareness to smart meters, or other technologies.

Rather, we must learn to think of digital technologies holistically and systemically in relation to ecosystems and territorial metabolisms.

So, can we use digital transformation spatially and systemically to create sustainable territorial metabolisms and establish holistic regenerative systems?

Can we use transition-oriented digital transformation as a tool to create not only a carbon-neutral future, but even a climate-positive one? Can we create a purposeful digital transition for territorial regeneration?

7 Grulois, Tosi, and Crosas: "Designing Territorial Metabolism: Barcelona, Brussels, and Venice."

8 "Biocapacity measures the capacity of ecosystems to produce the biological materials we use and to absorb the wastes we generate, using current management schemes and technologies." In: Planet Report.

9 Hails: "Living Planet Report 2006."

There are some pioneering international cities and regions that are already demonstrating how artificial intelligence and machine learning, for example, can be used in urban regeneration processes to achieve sustainability goals and stay within 1.5 degrees of warming.[10]

It is not individual digital solutions, but rather entire digital systems that are shaping not only physical space at the local level, but spatial changes to entire spatial systems in large-scale territories.

Examples here include mobility as a service, ICT-enabled renewable energy generation in smart grids, ICT-enabled food production, or automated driving. These territorial, digital technologies have the greatest potential to bring about large-scale transformation.

Because of their high complexity, they must be carefully planned and spatially integrated into the territory in question in an interdisciplinary manner.

System complexity is quite specifically applicable to territorial contexts. It maps the holistic approach of a territorial metabolism—that large-scale regions are subject to—in a cascade of complex processes during which material and energy flows are translated into spatial systems.[11] Therefore, for a healthy territorial metabolism, we should consider digital innovations and incorporate technological changes into the design of regeneration processes.[12]

What is important here is to avoid possible rebound effects, for example, to avoid negative consequences for biodiversity, or to ensure that the resources used to gain biocapacity do not in turn damage the footprint.

Finally, we are confronted with a rapidly changing and increasingly uncertain present, in which planning and design have become even more important than before. In this context, the speed of digital innovation has already exceeded the cycles of urban and territorial development. Therefore, in the digital age, fundamentally new patterns of thinking and planning are needed to meet the demands of the increasing speed of disruption. We also need new approaches to develop the necessary agility for an uncertain future—one that is sustainable and designed for the long term despite the dynamics of change.

10 Güleş, and Schweitzer: "Künstliche Intelligenz Und Stadtentwicklung." Informationen zur Raumentwicklung.

11 Pollo, , and Trane: "Adaptation, Mitigation, and Smart Urban Metabolism towards the Ecological Transition."

12 Shach-Pinsly: "Digital Urban Regeneration and Its Impact on Urban Renewal Processes and Development: Editorial."

Last but not least, we need to ask ourselves what ethical and legal arrangements might enable us to use digital transformation for the benefit of society and ecosystems.

Such developments should avoid power asymmetries, spatial frag-mentation, and displacement. If we can close material and energy loops of the carbon-intensive techno-sphere and put digital technologies at the service of territorial transition processes to significantly increase social and ecosystem value at the territorial level, we will be taking a good step toward securing the lives of all future planetary inhabitants.

VIII.

Notions

The process of territorial transition is complex in all its aspects, in terms of time loops, agents, and space. In this chapter the complexity of territorial transition is addressed in six core notions. The notions are described in a text and illustrated with territorial sections. Different approaches to the transition are shown in student projects from the two universities École nationale supérieure d'architecture de Versailles and Graz University of Technology. The projects present speculative, bold spatial design thinking but also concrete spatial strategies and process designs for the transition towards a climate-neutral future.

This chapter represents the future generation's perspective as a playful, experimental approach to territorial transition. It is an invitation to integrate speculative designs and spatial experiments as testing labs in the real world. It reminds us of the importance of implementing a culture of failure in order to achieve critical innovations for the territorial transition.

Scale

Transition

Territory

Platform

Resources

Uncertainty

Scale

Defining the unit of a strategic action and spatial design is decisive for its systemic integration. Territorial projects are developed in a multi-scalar dynamic. They move constantly between strategic aims, quantitative climate mitigation measures, and small-scale interventions translating the strategic aims into spatial qualities. Scale thus becomes a tool to decide, design, measure, evaluate, and relate systems to each other.

Designing ecology-related systems at a territorial scale is a key element for transition. It is not an abstract, generic unit but it is strongly bound to the eco-systemic reach of resources, such as water, energy, food, biodiversity, etc.

Scale

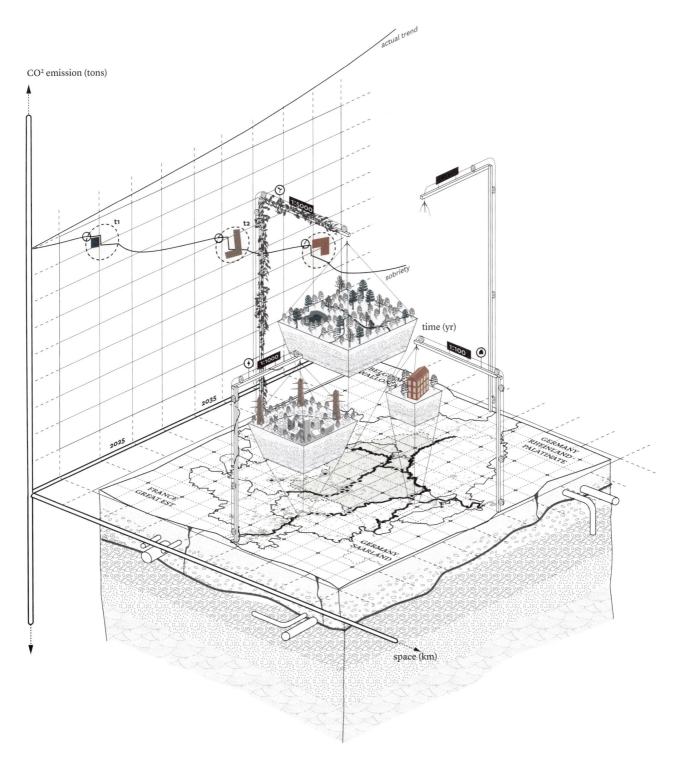

Fig. 80: Scale and territory

Scale

The insects

Project details
Location: Hesperange (LU)
Student: Thomas Breton

The site is located between a residential district and a forested area in the south of Luxembourg. Forests are central to meeting our zero-carbon goal, however, this one is currently in poor condition. One of the reasons for this is the presence of insects which attack the trees and cause them to dry out. Depending on the species, insects either multiply or tend to die out in a few years. The chains between insects, plants, and animals are therefore broken. At the edge of the big city, sites associated with agroforestry could function as reserves with the aim of large-scale re-establishment of various insects. The interplay of scales, from the very small to the very large—the metropolis—is nourished by the corridor projects and the numerous blue and green networks of recent years.

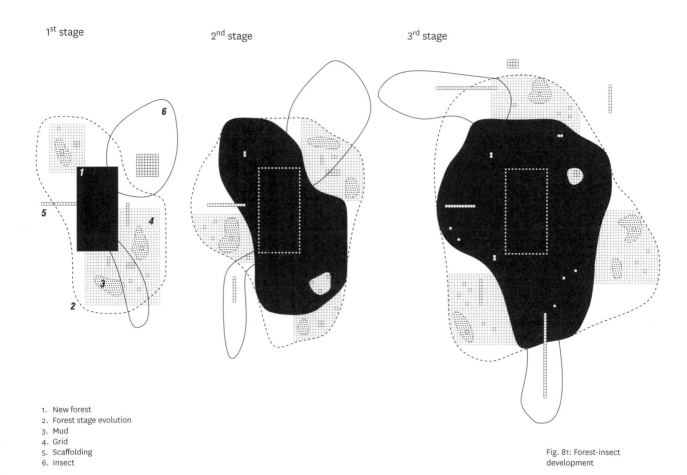

1. New forest
2. Forest stage evolution
3. Mud
4. Grid
5. Scaffolding
6. Insect

Fig. 81: Forest-insect development

140

Scale

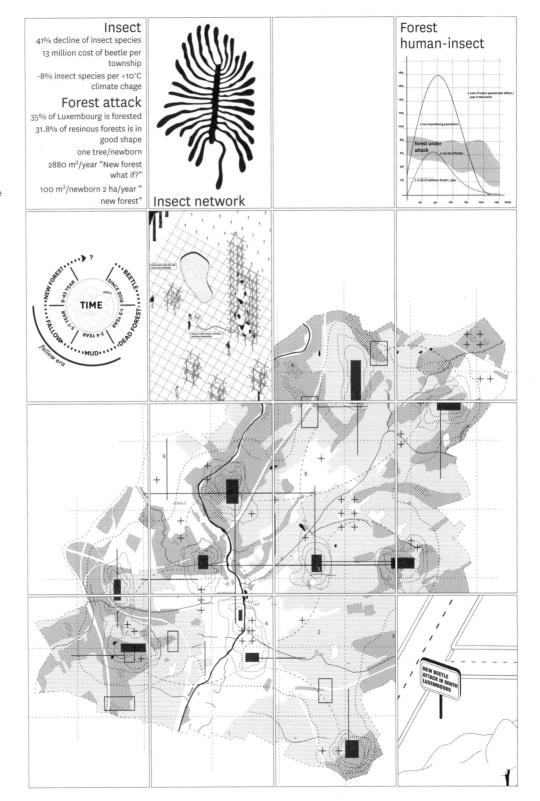

Fig. 82: Insects and forest relationship data
Fig. 83 Insect network 1/0.1e
Fig. 84: Tree attack graph

Fig. 85: Time process development of forest
Fig. 86: Zoom of the scaffolding installation
Fig. 87: Map of the interventions

1. Urban area
2. Field
3. Forest
4. Forest attack
5. New forest
6. Forest evolution
7. Insect connection
8. Scaffolding

Fig. 88: Zoom of the future scenario

Office to go

Shopping malls are converted into co-working spaces in order to reduce cross-border commuter flows and prevent CO^2 emissions. This creates a spatial network of flexible office spaces in the border regions.

Challenge

Luxembourg is experiencing a strong cross-border commuter flow, mainly from Belgium and France into Luxembourg City. One main reason behind this is the cheap fuel, which has resulted in a high load of motorized individual traffic, carbon emissions, and environmental pollution. Entry restrictions during the pandemic led to co-working spaces being created at the border to accommodate the employees who were not able to enter Luxembourg. This significantly reduced traffic between the border and Luxembourg City. This project combines this development with another factor generating cross-border flows: The existence of large malls with additional gas stations. These are in border areas of Luxembourg and are by definition mono-functional, with the result that their attractivity depends on the availability of cheap gas.

Strategy

The project addresses the transition of the mobility sector by introducing a decentralized network of co-working spaces located at the border and based on the concept of converting shopping malls into satellite offices. The growth of e-commerce accelerated by Covid-19 and the associated decline of traditional retail raises the question of whether shopping malls as mega structures will become obsolete. This approach prioritizes shopping malls with a good connection to the railway and cycling infrastructure in order to enable carbon-reduced commuting. Additionally, the green-blue connections and eco-systemic value of the surroundings of these collaborative office spaces are deeply integrated into the transformation. The ground, previously sealed to accommodate motorized parking, is opened up. By following this approach, cross-border commuter traffic and CO^2 emissions can be significantly reduced and the large-scale systemic integration and hybridization of high-quality networks, such as the cycling network and blue-green network, can serve as an approach towards territorial transition.

Scale

Project details
Student: Mendi Kocis

Fig. 89: Territorial strategy for spatial network of flexible office spaces, Border interface: from shopping to remote working and business meetings.

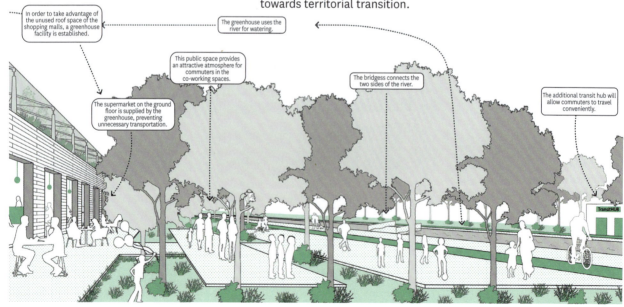

Scale

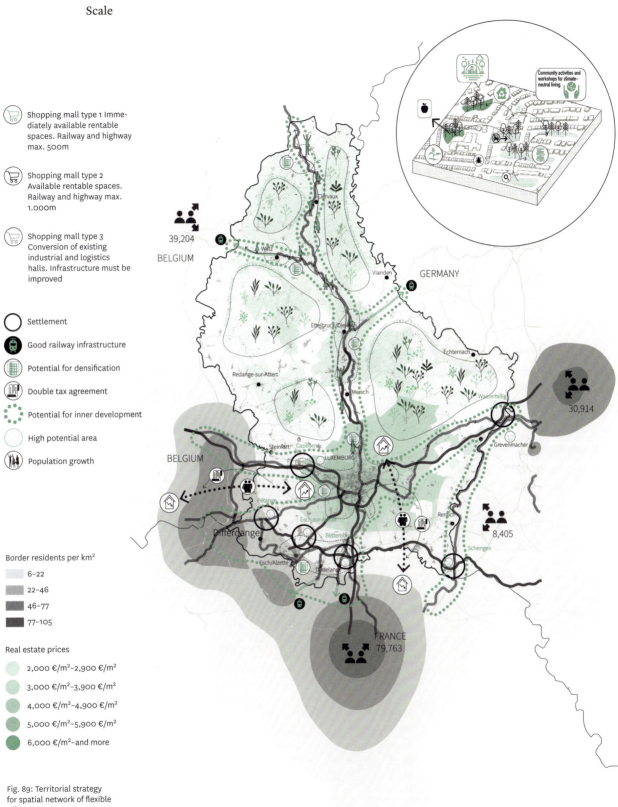

Fig. 89: Territorial strategy for spatial network of flexible office spaces

Transition

Transition is a process of gradual change from one situation to another. The challenge humanity is facing today is the transition from a fossil-fuel economy to a post-carbon society. The transition process relates the actions to be undertaken to the time required and aims not only for a quantitative but also for a qualitative transformation. The design of this process towards CO_2 neutrality is important and needs to be organized on a continuous basis, step by step, in order to avoid a hard social, economic, or ecological shock.

Even if different forces are constantly reshaping our environment, transition is not an endless process; it has a beginning and an end. Transition is a process that starts from the necessity and urgency of climate-oriented territorial change. To reaching the common goal of CO_2 neutrality it offers quantitative metrics but more importantly strategical spatial approaches, which are both climate-oriented and large-scale. Transition combines the climate potentials with spatial qualities and creates multi-scalar, measurable added value to make possible a long-term co-existence of all species.

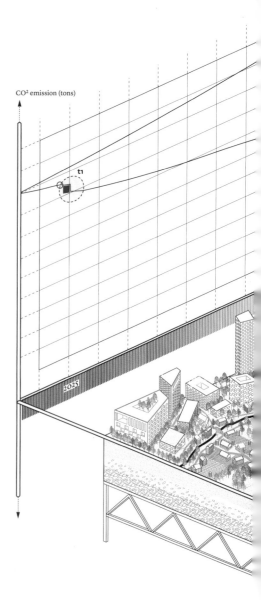

Transition

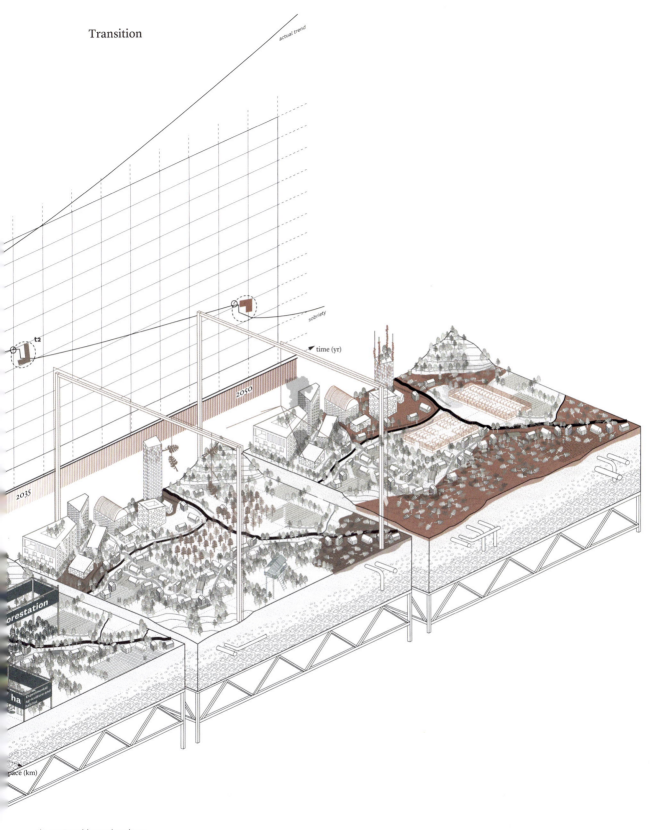

Fig. 91: Transition and territory

Marshes attack

The Cattenom nuclear power plant, a fantastic cathedral of nuclear power with four large parabolic chimneys, has a direct impact on its environment. In addition to the impacts of pollution, the plumes of smoke and the wetland buffer zone located along the Moselle River make it the preferred migratory path of some bird species. The surrounding countryside, composed essentially of forests and marshes, makes usual CO^2 calculations irrelevant and begs the question of what should become of the territory when the plant is decommissioned—and dismantled—as is scheduled for 2040. The large forest that surrounds it is very different from typical forests in Luxembourg: The many oak trees are used in the large-scale production of wine barrels in the Bordeaux region. The profitability of this production is such that it is not a problem that half of the trees are not used. Another point to consider is that the area is also subject to major flooding.

There are around 30 years left until 2050, time which can be used to experiment and activate a space that embraces the uncertainty of the ecological transition around a convergence of partners and networks that are compacting and evolving to allow the site to be a regional compensator.

Transition

Project details
Location: Cattenon, Basse-Ham (FR)
Student: Aymerick Brouez

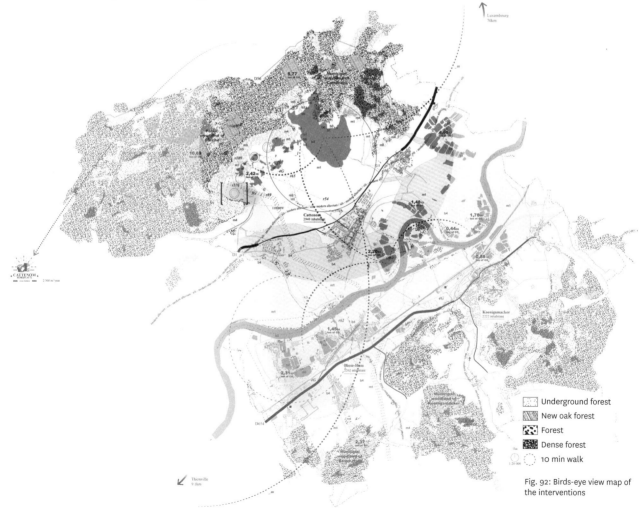

Fig. 92: Birds-eye view map of the interventions

Transition

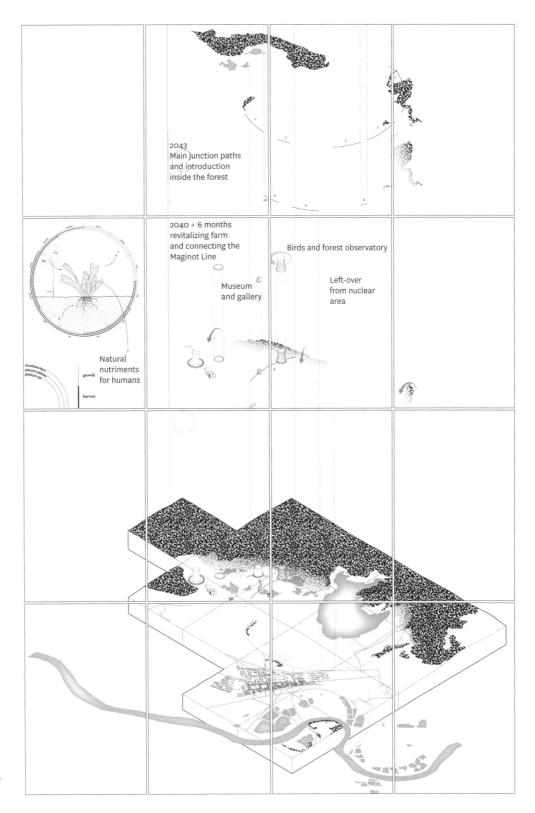

Fig. 93: Remediation plants scheme

Fig. 94: Reconfiguration strategy over the process of marshes attack

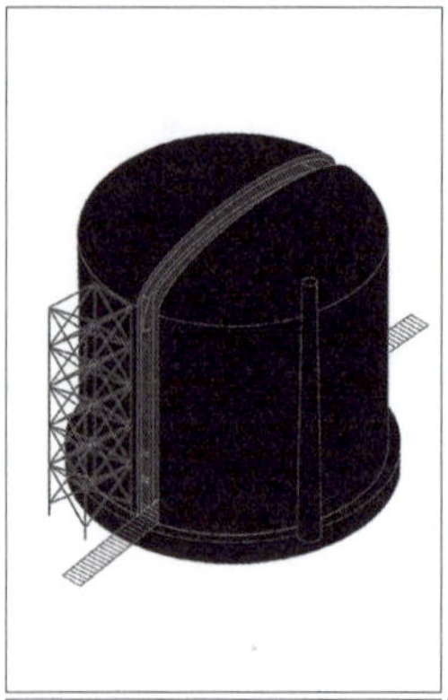

Transition

Inaccessible nature

Re-establishing the dialogue between the diffuse city and its "living networks" is one of the essential issues. The project centers on the need to transform certain industrial sites, the requirement to de-densify and how these are related to both urban growth and the fragility of natural environments. Urban corridors, which also represent network corridors—with little grids—must be reinvented.

Project details
Location: Luxembourg (LU),
Student: Alizée Bearzi

Fig. 95: Nuclear island

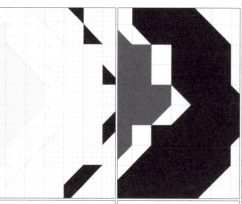

■ Water: 10.5%
■ Moritius forest: 31%
▨ Open forest: 25.5%
□ Fallow: 10%
▦ Built zone: 18.5%
▨ Vineyards: 4.5%

Fig. 96: Defenition of the territorial strategy area

Fig. 97: Luxembourg site mapping

Fig. 98: Mutated site mapping

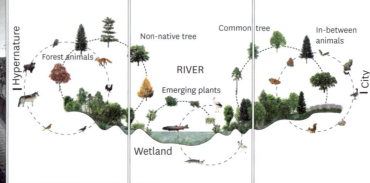

Logic trasnformation

Possible scenarios include the renaturation of the banks and the immediate surroundings together with the management of the partially transformed logistics and the establishment of new local productive activities on the unused hillsides. A changing climate makes the territory favorable to the growth of lavender, for example, with the result that the territory can reveal new forms of production.

Fig. 99: Fallow land scenario

Fig. 100: Ecosystem mechanism scheme

Project details
Location: Trier, Konz, Igel, Wasserliesch (DE)
Student: Caitlin Lam Tze Ting

Fig. 101: Fallow land scenario

150

Transition

Project details
Location: Tendel (LU)
Student: Cécile Kermaïdic

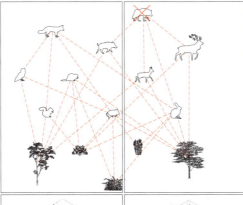

Animals as keystone

The nature reserve "Schoofsbësch" raises the question of which animals play a central role within the forests, and which in fact have a problematic effect on this environment. The area stands out due to its collaborative treatment of water networks: a large, isolated but technologically innovative plant connects around ten municipalities. This study points to a problem of compatibility between urbanity and wildness.

Fig. 102: Forest ecosystem network scheme

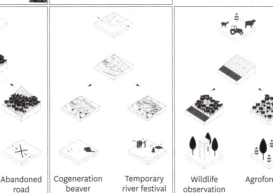
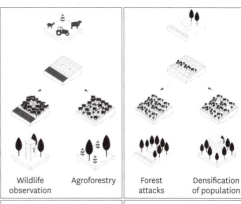

Ecological bridges | Abandoned road | Cogeneration beaver | Temporary river festival | Wildlife observation | Agroforestry | Forest attacks | Densification of population

Fig. 103: Road strategies
Fig. 104: River and waste strategies
Fig. 105: Agriculture and pasture strategies

Project details
Location: Luxembourg (LU)
Student: Soohye Jeong

Landscape reconnection

Nestling between plateaus and hills, the site is seldomly frequented by inhabitants. On the hillsides, the houses are organized in a network. Below, the isolated sewage treatment plant treats the water of the network "in terminus". A reflection, developed around the synergy of the networks could allow the site to reintegrate the river as an active landscape.

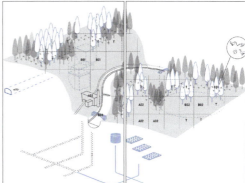

Fig. 106: Underground water system strategy

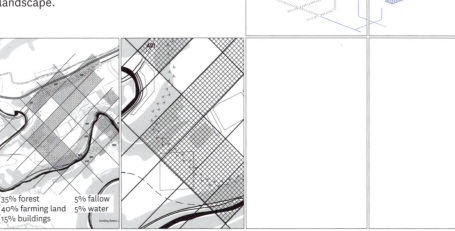

35% forest   5% fallow
40% farming land   5% water
15% buildings

Fig. 107: Territorial analysis of land uses
Fig. 108: Zoom of territorial land uses

151

Transition

Fuel for life

Reactivating obsolete fuel infrastructure to foster the energy transition and enable the reuse of gas stations to overcome fuel tourism.

Project details
Student: Carina Mazelle

Challenge

The project addresses the uncertainties involved in the transition of the mobility sector by converting obsolete fuel infrastructures. The settlement Wasserbillig—at the German border—suffers from commuter traffic, heavy motorized traffic and especially gas tourism. This has serious consequences for Wasserbillig's spatial appearance and image. Due to the low taxes on gas fuel prices in Luxembourg, twelve gas stations are clustered in one street. These gas stations, including car parking, are responsible for sealed space and stimulate even more car traffic. Although the settlement is compact and accessible by foot, Wasserbillig's public space is mainly designed for motorized traffic and not for walkability or active mobility. The main roads create barriers that prevent residential areas from accessing green and recreational spaces.

Strategy

Gas stations are transformed into sustainable mobility hubs that serve as meeting points with new additional uses. Unused parking lots can be environmentally upgraded. Green cross-connections and corridors break down barriers and strengthen paths for active mobility. Furthermore, the strategy provides Park&Go or Park&Bike areas at the city entrance to calm traffic. Large-scale green corridors connected to the waterside promote biodiversity. The Moselle River is integrated into the city, activated, and made accessible. Water can contribute to cooling the city center and be used as recreational space to reduce mobility demands for leisure. Unused parking lots can be unsealed and climatically activated to absorb CO^2. Transport resources and infrastructure can be repurposed, e.g., as meeting places, learning centers, and co-working spaces. Parking areas and streets are reclaimed and can be actively used by the population. The uses of the ground floor zones can expand into the public space and increase the liveliness of the streets. This will lead to more meeting spaces and thus to more active mobility.

Fig. 109: Establishing a large-scale green belt in Luxembourg as a dense energy network along borders

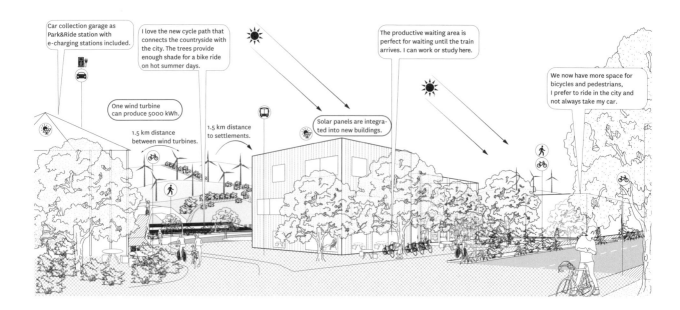

Transition

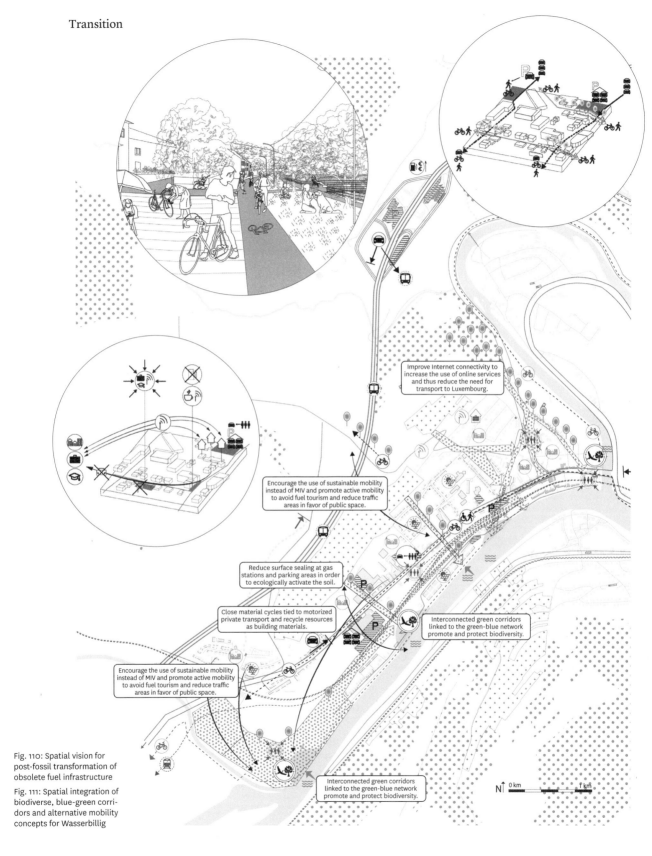

Fig. 110: Spatial vision for post-fossil transformation of obsolete fuel infrastructure

Fig. 111: Spatial integration of biodiverse, blue-green corridors and alternative mobility concepts for Wasserbillig

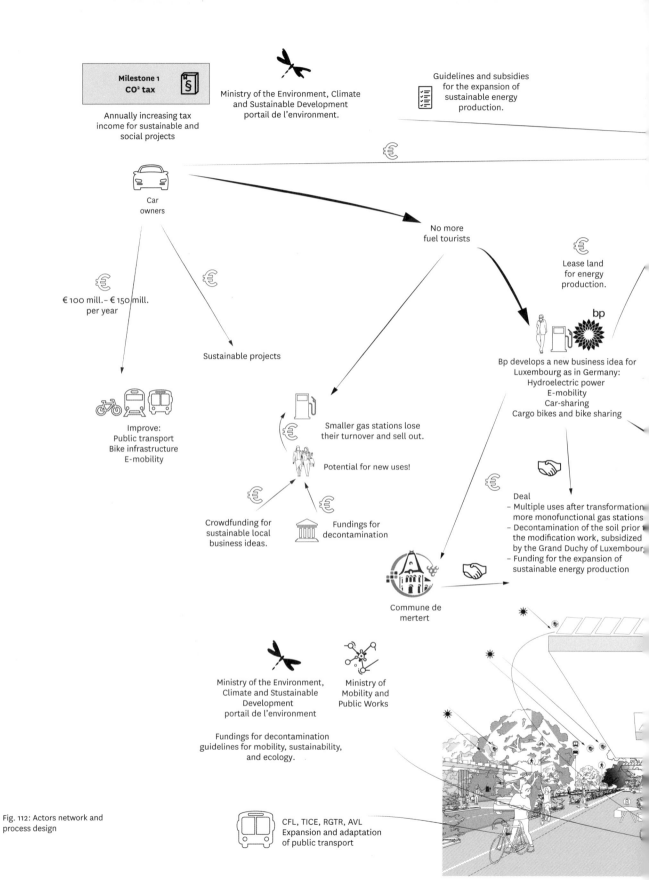

Fig. 112: Actors network and process design

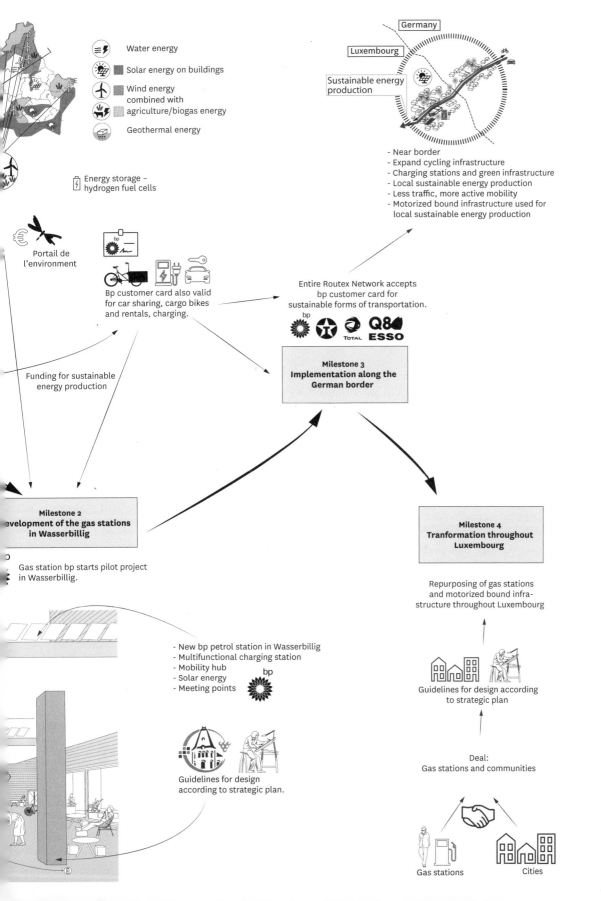

Territory

Any form of action in ecology, economy, or social relations (human and more-than-human) is related to specific geography, with its specific systemic and often elastic boundaries. The complex systemic relations of any activity to the ground describes a territory. It is not a random piece of land but is always deeply related to the specific place with its soil, resources, ecosystems, climate, and other agents. Based on ecology, these aspects define the size and the potential of the territory's structuring elements.

A territorial project is not limited to a single place defined by the property line but situates the project site within a wider area connected to ecological systems and their metabolism. The metabolism of a site's system does not end at geopolitical or legal boundaries but continues beyond them.

Designing and structuring the territory with its large-scale, trans-border networks, systems, and spaces becomes a project of ecological transition. Territorial projects are aiming not only for adaptation to but also mitigation of climate change, increasing the number of site-specific potential uses and preventing CO^2 emissions with a non-hierarchical approach towards ecological systems.

Territory

Fig. 113: Territory

Territory

Trinational

Project details
Location: Schengen (LU), Perl (DE), Apach (FR)
Student: Roman Le Cornec

Three villages are situated adjacent to the border: Schengen, a wealthy Luxembourg village, is a riverside resort renowned for its water and wine; Perl is a German village with generous housing estates existing alongside businesses and industrial zones; and Apach is a French village on the decline with a disused railway yard. The three national identities are cultivated through key concepts: a pastiche of the Eiffel Tower, beer cellar, and euroshop. The Moselle River creates a strong natural border with an island and a range of infrastructure at the end of the adjoining regions forming a succession of barriers. Occasionally, France and Luxembourg collaborate in their water management, with both using the French water treatment plant, which creates a cross-border hinterland. The site is also an important cross-roads: its tourist attraction and the presence of a gas station at the entrance of the village make it a very problematic node from the point of view of the carbon footprint. The numerous floods submerge the lock more and more regularly and the river banks, which are located in the risk areas, are not or hardly used. The provision of a part of these spaces exceeding 10% of the site could serve as a trinational platform connecting the networks.

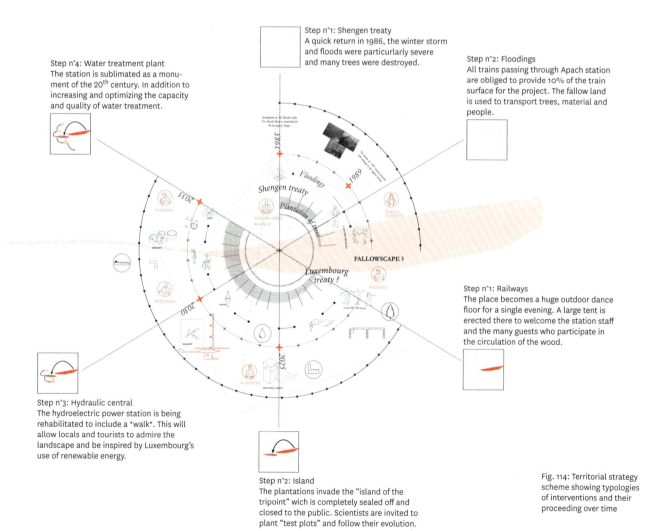

Step n°4: Water treatment plant
The station is sublimated as a monument of the 20th century. In addition to increasing and optimizing the capacity and quality of water treatment.

Step n°1: Shengen treaty
A quick return in 1986, the winter storm and floods were particurlarly severe and many trees were destroyed.

Step n°2: Floodings
All trains passing through Apach station are obliged to provide 10% of the train surface for the project. The fallow land is used to transport trees, material and people.

Step n°3: Hydraulic central
The hydroelectric power station is being rehabilitated to include a *walk*. This will allow locals and tourists to admire the landscape and be inspired by Luxembourg's use of renewable energy.

Step n°1: Railways
The place becomes a huge outdoor dance floor for a single evening. A large tent is erected there to welcome the station staff and the many guests who participate in the circulation of the wood.

Step n°2: Island
The plantations invade the "island of the tripoint" wich is completely sealed off and closed to the public. Scientists are invited to plant "test plots" and follow their evolution.

Fig. 114: Territorial strategy scheme showing typologies of interventions and their proceeding over time

160

Territory

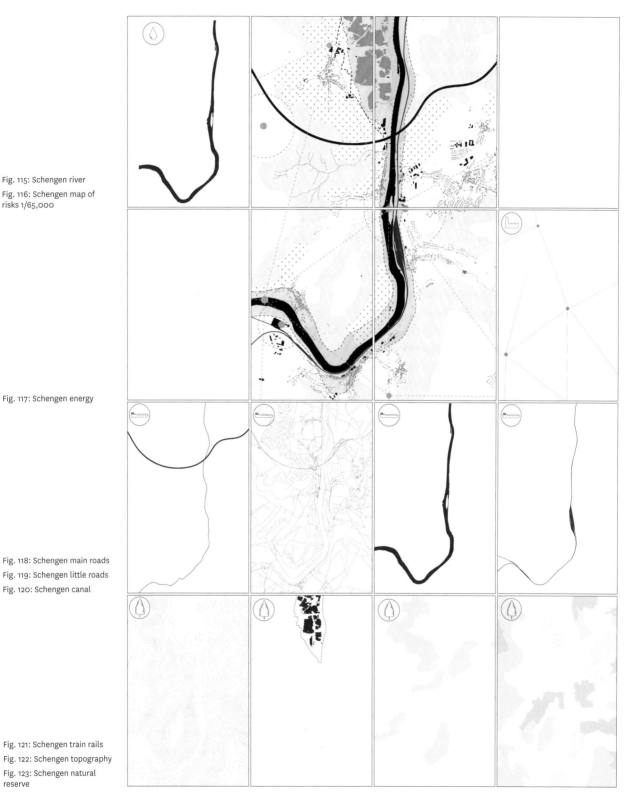

Fig. 115: Schengen river
Fig. 116: Schengen map of risks 1/65,000

Fig. 117: Schengen energy

Fig. 118: Schengen main roads
Fig. 119: Schengen little roads
Fig. 120: Schengen canal

Fig. 121: Schengen train rails
Fig. 122: Schengen topography
Fig. 123: Schengen natural reserve

Territory

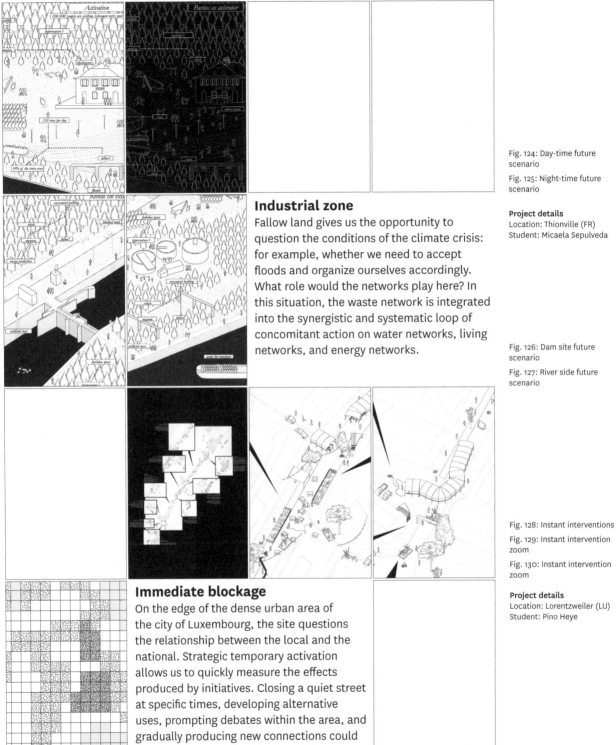

Industrial zone
Fallow land gives us the opportunity to question the conditions of the climate crisis: for example, whether we need to accept floods and organize ourselves accordingly. What role would the networks play here? In this situation, the waste network is integrated into the synergistic and systematic loop of concomitant action on water networks, living networks, and energy networks.

Fig. 124: Day-time future scenario
Fig. 125: Night-time future scenario

Project details
Location: Thionville (FR)
Student: Micaela Sepulveda

Fig. 126: Dam site future scenario
Fig. 127: River side future scenario

Immediate blockage
On the edge of the dense urban area of the city of Luxembourg, the site questions the relationship between the local and the national. Strategic temporary activation allows us to quickly measure the effects produced by initiatives. Closing a quiet street at specific times, developing alternative uses, prompting debates within the area, and gradually producing new connections could have an impact on the whole mobility system.

Fig. 128: Instant interventions
Fig. 129: Instant intervention zoom
Fig. 130: Instant intervention zoom

Project details
Location: Lorentzweiler (LU)
Student: Pino Heye

Fig. 129: Fallowland mapping

162

Territory

Project details
Location: Arlon (BE),
Steinfort (LU)
Student: Salila Shou

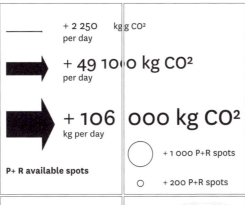

Fig. 132: CO_2 emission per week for 20.000 workers crossing 2x per day

Transborder archipelago

The site is an opportunity to rethink how synergies can be formed between water networks and other networks, in particular transport networks, energy networks and networks for living. Experimenting with a new side by side and above and below relationship can lead to a new metropolitan mesh that might be multiplied and weave an active territory, adding value by a tactical approach instead of an urban strategy.

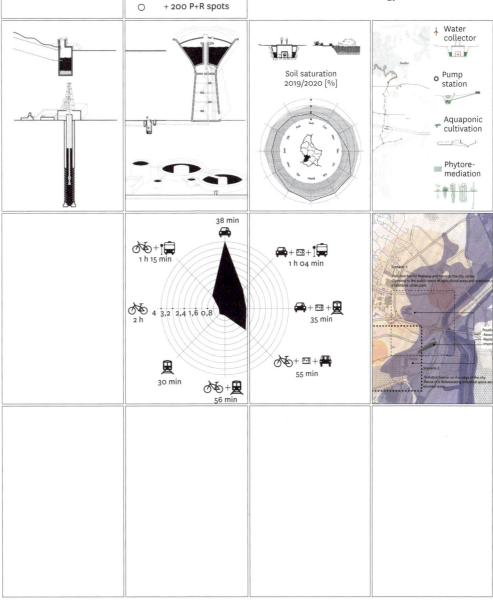

Fig. 133: Water treatment detail

Fig. 134: Soil saturation quantity

Fig. 135: River side future scenario

- Urban heat islands increase in Co 2-3
- Urban heat islands increase in Co 3-4
- Agricultural lands
- Low average flood risk
- Flood risk

Fig. 136: CO_2 emission per person (kg)

Fig. 137: Territorial strategy

Mobile medical care loop

Project details
Student: Carola Hilgert

Mobile medical care in rural territories as a strategy for avoiding additional construction.

Challenge
With its direct connection to the Mosel River, Remich is a hotspot for tourists, but it is also greatly affected by commuter transit traffic in the direction of Luxembourg City. Most of the border territory lacks mobility, social, and health infrastructure, especially for an aging population. Access to specialized medical and health care creates individual mobility needs and takes 30 min by car or 60 min by bus. Most people opt for private transport since it is quicker, despite all the environmental consequences.

Strategy
The strategy proposes improving access to health care in rural regions instead of building additional medical infrastructure. Collective express e-buses connect the rural territories with the nearest hospital in Luxembourg City in a dense frequency in order to reduce the need for the individual mobility responsible for CO_2 emissions. In addition, a mobile healthcare hub with mobile units (bus and boat) serves the entire rural territory. For medical care, mobile facilities are installed to provide routine treatment for patients. Living conditions in villages along the medical supply belt in the rural territory become more attractive and transition towards becoming a climate-friendly environment. In bigger settlements, poly-functional multi-modal hubs provide alternative mobility infrastructure for residents, such as carpools and car sharing. Mobile medical care, or express buses to the hospital break the dependency on individual traffic.

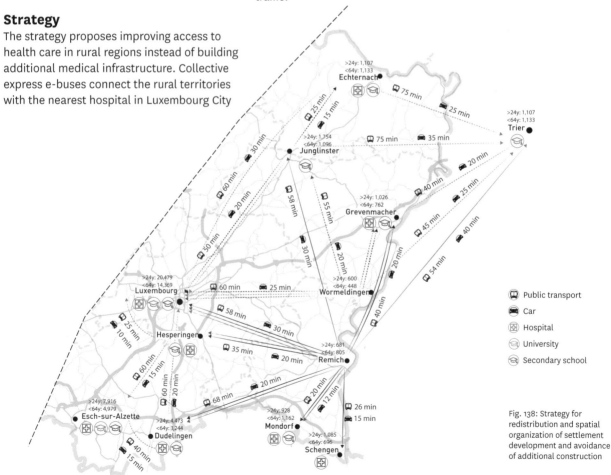

Fig. 138: Strategy for redistribution and spatial organization of settlement development and avoidance of additional construction

Territory

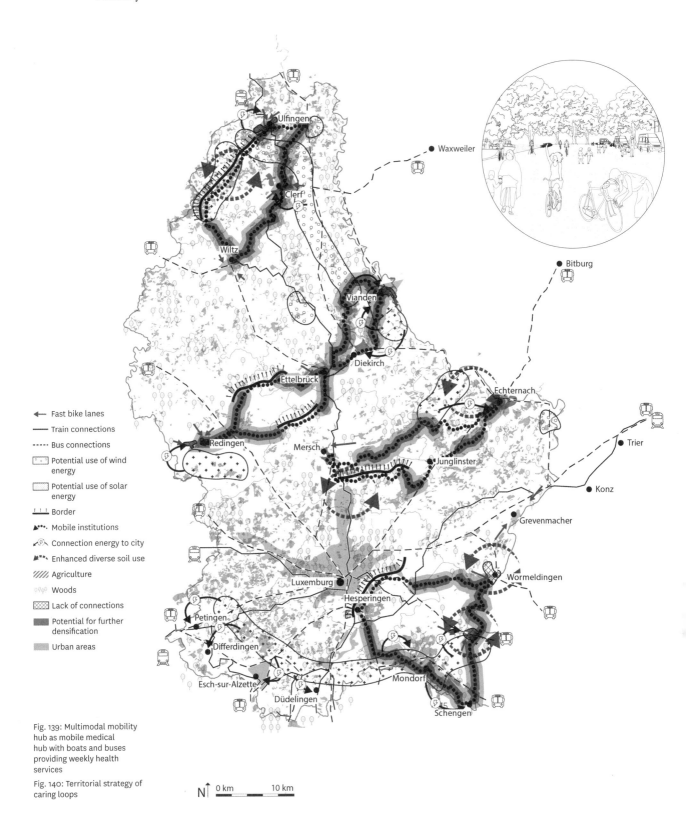

Fig. 139: Multimodal mobility hub as mobile medical hub with boats and buses providing weekly health services

Fig. 140: Territorial strategy of caring loops

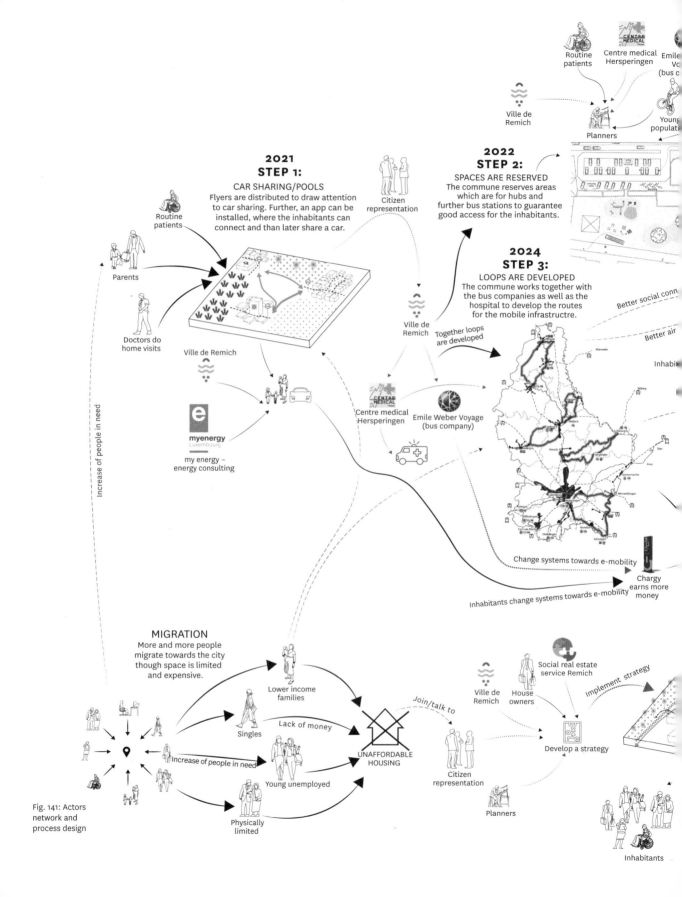

Fig. 141: Actors network and process design

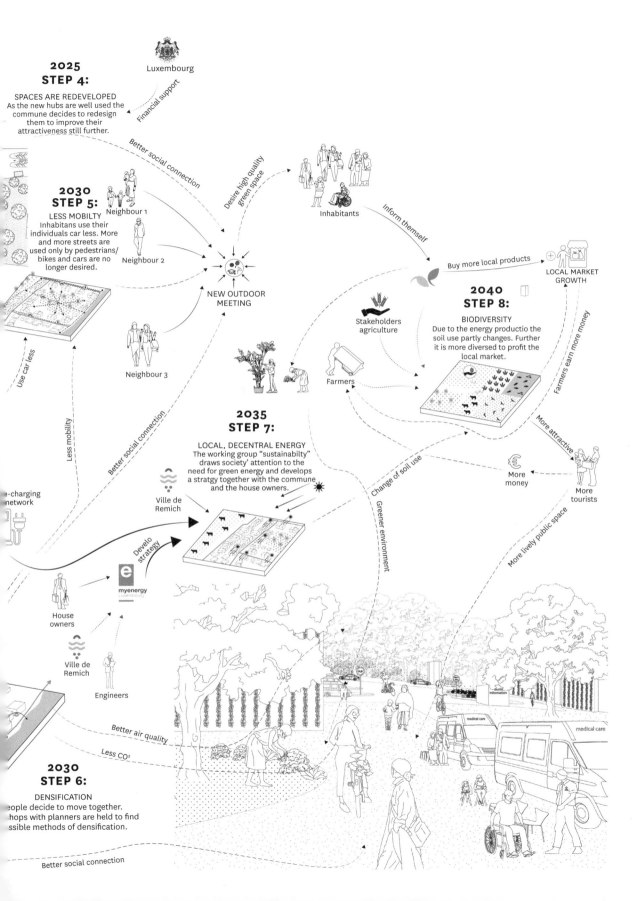

Platform

Because of the discipline's fragmentation and the need to shift systems towards frugality and deep change, transformative actions can only emerge with joint forces in a non-hierarchical co-creation process. A platform is an organizational structure that operates in a networked, collective, horizontal co-creation process between a diversity of actors and agents who share a common mindset or collective goal. New developments call for interdisciplinary, mixed teams where actors represent all different interests of society. A dense network of collaboration helps expand disciplinary boundaries, avoid silo thinking, and create alliances. This collaborative approach releases hidden innovation potentials of alliances to address the wicked problems of climate change.

Being part of a platform in the territorial transition process means embracing a mode which prioritizes the collective climate commons over individual authorship in order to horizontally co-create added value not only for clients but for all human and more-than-human agents.

Platform

Fig. 142: Platform and territory

171

Fragile nature

Project details
Location: Rambrouch (LU)
Student: Loris Peziere

To the north of the city and at the end of the water reservoir system of the Esch-sur-Sûre dam, the site, characterized by its beauty, seems to be essentially composed of emptiness. A series of villages is structured around a sparsely inhabited countryside, large forests, and livestock pasture. The territory is, however, subject to environmental problems: The forests, particularly affected in recent years, are likely to be impacted by forest fires and the variation of the water level jeopardizes the control of the fragile natural space.

Located at the outer limit of the metropolitan area, this site has the potential to become a natural resource that can help the entire agglomeration reach its zero-carbon goal.

The study of different actors and their network serves as a testing ground for finding an appropriate project granulometry. In an initial stage, the networking of identified resources and needs will allow us to identify specific action scenarios that could then become systemic.

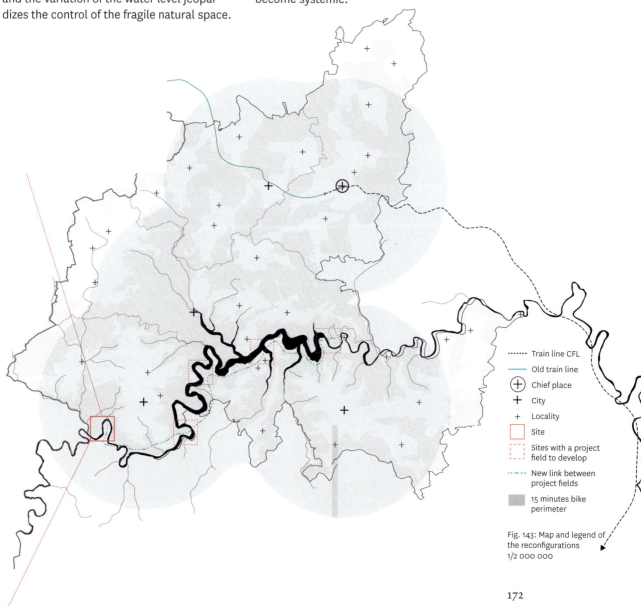

Fig. 143: Map and legend of the reconfigurations
1/2 000 000

Platform

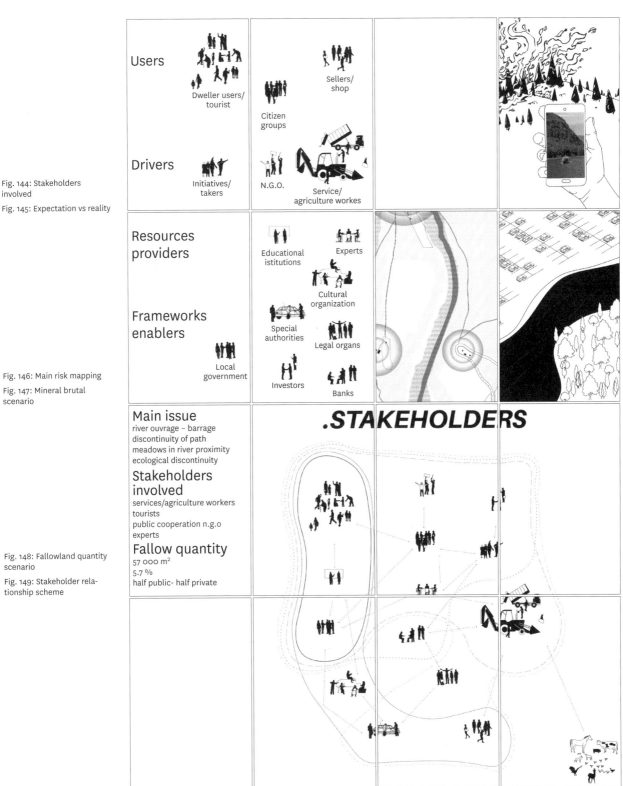

Fig. 144: Stakeholders involved

Fig. 145: Expectation vs reality

Fig. 146: Main risk mapping

Fig. 147: Mineral brutal scenario

Fig. 148: Fallowland quantity scenario

Fig. 149: Stakeholder relationship scheme

Stay up

Collective, bottom-up activation of vacant housing units to provide affordable housing while reducing urban sprawl and further sealing of green space.

Challenge

Seen within a European context, real estate prices in Luxembourg are very high, both in terms of rent and property prices. On average 35 percent of income is spent on housing. Especially in the region of Luxembourg City and in the south of Luxembourg prices correlate mostly with the income structure and with motorized traffic infrastructure. Surprisingly, there is no correlation between real estate prices and carbon-reduced railway infrastructure. In Esch-sur-Alzette the situation directly at the railway tracks is the socially weakest and with the highest percentage of sealed ground. It is also here that CO_2 emissions and noise pollution are at their highest.

Strategy

The project tackles the transition process by activating resources and actor networks. It embraces uncertainties and proposes alternative multi-ownership solutions for active and electric mobility in order to reduce CO_2 emissions. The project aims to densify inner development along high-performance railway lines in order to ensure accessibility to carbon-reduced mobility and prevent additional sealing of ground. The existing buildings can be used as affordable housing in a collective re-using and renovation process. The project follows the concept of establishing the incentive of a coop system in which low-income individuals renovate buildings step by step and thus increase the value of the property. In exchange they pay only a minimum of rent to live there. With this approach the different actors and agencies are connected to a platform which enables careful use of resources and significantly reduces carbon emissions by preventing additional construction activities.

Project details
Student: Marie-Theres Schwaighofer

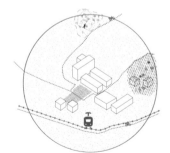

Creating a city that functions entirely without private cars, but can rely on active mobility, public transport and multiple-ownership solutions to function in order to bring down CO_2 emissions to a minimum.

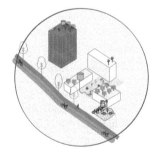

Building must amplify greenery, and are to be equipped with small scale energy sources if possible to sustain themeselfs next to the development of a strict re-source-management plan and try to push occupancy to a maximum.

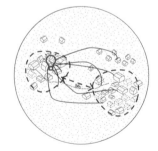

Implementing a strong relationship between the university and the city of Esch-sur-Alzette by becoming more a part of daily life, integrating research and knowledge in the City and have the Population participate.

Fig. 150: Strategy for collective, bottom-up activation of vacant housing

Platform

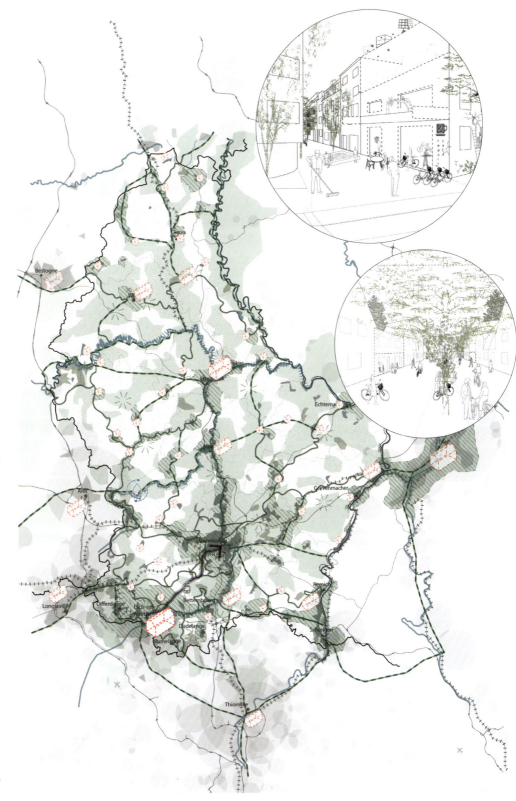

Re-activate housing project
Garage-activating project
Highspeed bike connection
Tram connection
Project/activate greenspace
Activated waterspace
Recreative greenspace
Protected area
Agriculture
Forest
Airport
Railway
River
National border
District border
City
Settlement

Fig. 152: Renovation and densification measures as potential for activating not only unused or underused housing but also improving public space

Fig. 153: Territorial development of affordable housing along green-blue high quality network

175

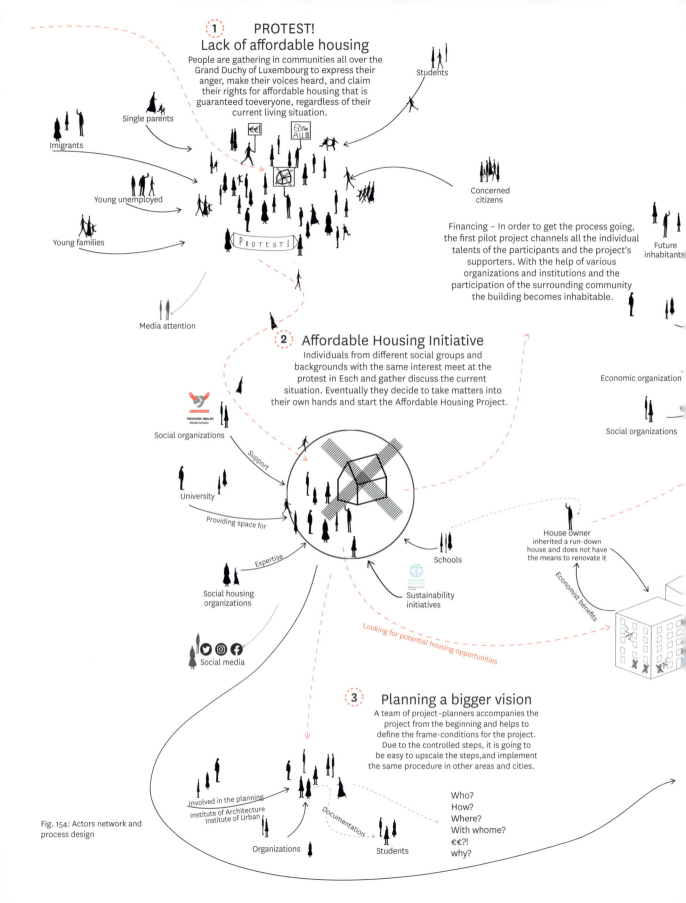

Fig. 154: Actors network and process design

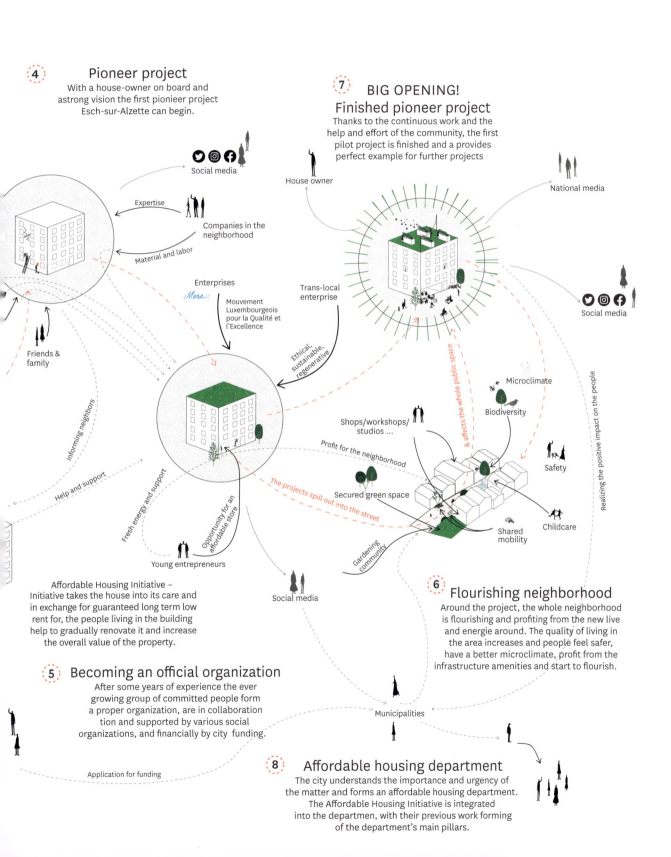

Resources

Humankind's global approach to consumptive patterns and economic growth is exceeding the planetary boundaries. This means that change needs to be based on a frugal use of resources. Reuse of material resources (urban mining) and activation of vacant, underused, or unused resources is an effective way to drive change towards circular systems.

Closing circular flows in the process of transition is key. But responsible design also means critically examining the need to build in general and thus not only questioning the use of resources but also exploiting the potential alternatives of reuse and conversion.

Resources

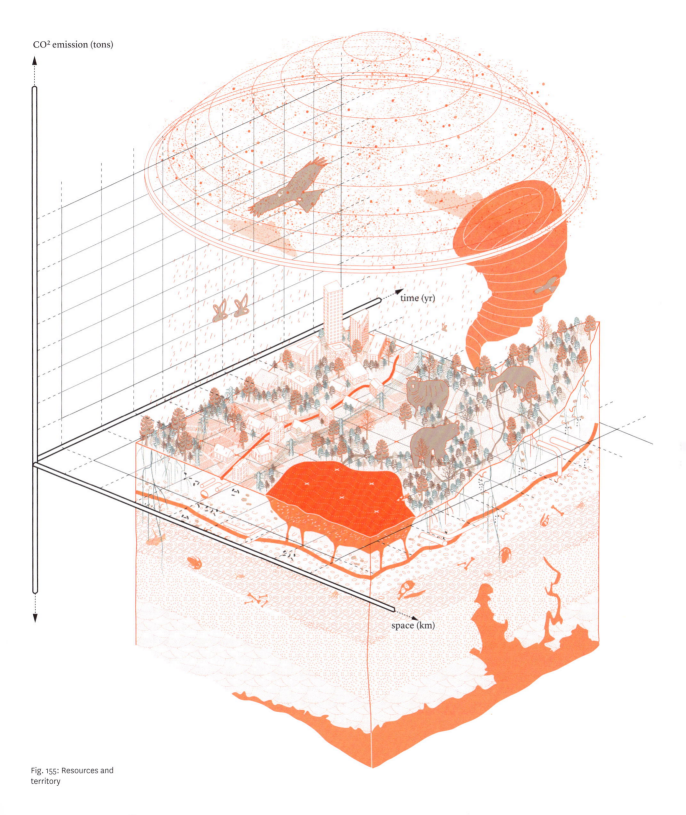

Fig. 155: Resources and territory

Resources

Project details
Location: Cattenon,
Koenigsmacker (FR)
Student: Louise Ciceri

Marshes

The first thing that comes to mind when you mention the name Cattenom is the French nuclear power plant located in Lorraine. However, to the northwest of it, the village that gave its name to the area unfolds in a landscape of marshes and immense flood zones, structured by the Moselle and by water infrastructure, such as the water treatment plant, dams, and locks. Studying the site reveals an important network of fishermen who face several problems. These are a change of temperature that has caused the water level to drop, an infrastructure deficiency and pollution of the water and soil, factors which have all led to a dramatic deterioration of fishing conditions in the area.

Despite the proximity of the nuclear power plant, the study area is less polluted than most of the Moselle River. As marshes store more CO^2 than forests, the site provides an ideal example of the carbon sink effect, and this could be exploited and multiplied.

"Ecology clearly is not the irruption of nature into the public space but the end of 'nature' as a concept that would allow us to sum up our relations to the world and pacify them." Facing Gaia, Bruno Latour

This place, redesigned around a synergy of water, fishing, and energy networks could become a compensatory resource that would allow for a slower renaturation of the surrounding sites which are highly polluted. It demonstrates broader territorial thinking that—in the context of the Covid-19 situation— opens up an immediate, tactical opportunity for action and provides an impetus for intergenerational fishing along the shoreline. Frustration has become an activator of slow city, of local loops, of mastery of the halieutic environments.

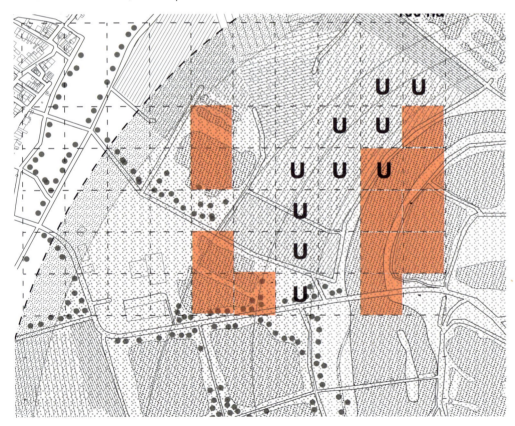

Fig. 156: Fallow land map
1/1 0000

182

Resources

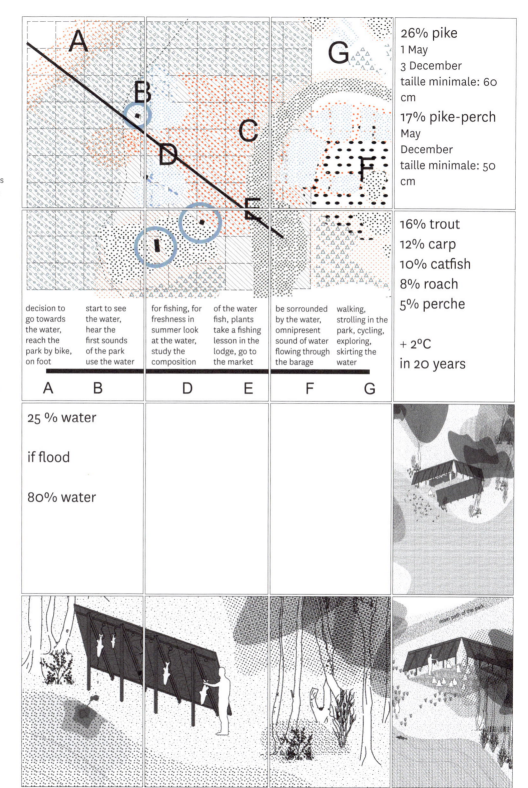

Fig. 157: Map of future actions
Fig. 158: Quantity of fish over the year

Fig. 159: Diversities of fish in the river

Fig. 160: Quantity of flood
Fig. 161: Zoom of a future scenario

Fig. 162: Zoom of a future scenario
Fig. 163: Zoom of a future scenario

183

Resources

The water plant

Within this small tourist town, the largest water plant, isolated and completely closed, dominates a series of infrastructures. By bringing together risk zones, flood perimeters, attraction factors, and nuisances linked to mass tourism, the small village in the heart of Luxembourg provides an example of a judicious intervention into the networks as part of which the actors powerfully reshape the territory.

Project details
Location: Bettembourg, Livange, Peppange (LU)
Student: Gaelle Dechenaux

713 400 kW each month with these two unlimited energy production mechanisms

€ 140 144 enough to finance the installation of 3 wind trees each month

total energy produced per month: **713 400 kW** with a total financial investment of: **€ 604 000** or 4 months to become profitable

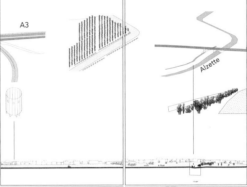

Fig. 164: Action impact quantity
Fig. 165: Action impact quantity
Fig. 166: Territorial section of actions

"green revolution"
20 bikes, 4 h a day: **300 kW per month and per gym, 6 months of electricity for 1 house** thanks to 12V per bycicle

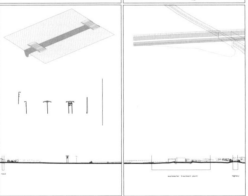

Fig. 167: Action impact quantity
Fig. 168: Territorial section of actions

"pavegen"
6 plates per m², can be installed on the floor of sports field, **1 footstep gives 5W**

Nocturnal river

The study makes it possible to see the river as a project opportunity, focusing on it at night, its uses, its frequentations, and its potential to generate a common life or even tourism. The concept of the night fallow is associated with a quiet and slower paced time and, by questioning the artificial lighting in public spaces, fundamentally addresses the management of energy networks.

Project details
Location: Luxembourg (LU)
Student: Suzanne Brigaud

Fig. 169: Action impact quantity

184

Resources

Project details
Location: Mertet (LU),
Langsur (DE)
Student: Rhita Adnane

Groundwater

The health of the forests in the area is worrying and climatic changes are likely to generate problems of water runoff. Analyzing the water networks, the living networks, and the energy networks could make it possible to draw up hypotheses about the storage of excess water which could also be beneficial to the sick forest.

Fig. 170: Territorial strategy axonometry

Fig. 171: Map of mobility emission

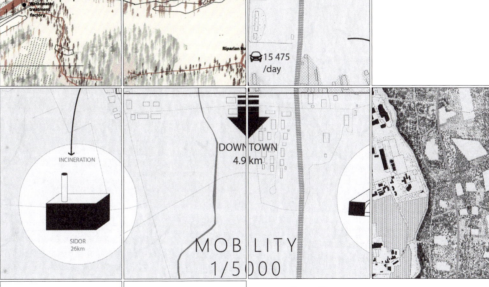

Fig. 172: Map of the fallow land

Project details
Location: Luxembourg,
Walferdange (LU)
Student: Maria Zboralska

Inner border

As a territory at risk of flooding, the question of transport networks echoes that of water and energy networks. The local authorities intend to develop gas networks in connection with the existing water treatment plant. The bridge and the abandoned banks are spaces that could become places of experimentation and an embodiment of zero carbon, at the crossroads of all practices.

Fig. 173: Water threatment mechanism

Resources

Project details
Student: Beatrice Wagner

Gourmet region

Regional organic agriculture is combined with culinary tourism to foster the creation of local socio-economic added value.

Challenge

The existing economic system in the North of Luxembourg is mono-functional. Over 80 percent of jobs are in the service sector, and the financial sector dominates. Luxembourg's financial center is one of the largest in the world and high investments are made in companies that exploit, process, and market oil, gas, or coal. Low taxes are responsible for high prices and a high number of commuters. Business tourism is an important industry, but there is little to no health tourism or leisure tourism, meaning that the population usually flies to long-distance vacation destinations. Luxembourg is also affected by the urban-rural divide. Tourist flows and thus the infrastructure is concentrated in the city. Small and medium-sized companies are closing and are being replaced by large hotels and chains. Further, a large part of the food required is imported from abroad and is responsible for significant CO^2 emissions. The agricultural land in the north is characterized by monoculture and contributes to the long-term damage of the soil and additional species extinction due to a focus on profit and pesticide use.

Strategy

The strategy proposed is to establish regional organic agriculture combined with gourmet tourism. In order to counteract the monofunctional economic structure the promotion of regional markets, organic agricultural production, and communication is suggested. The expansion of leisure tourism and the bicycle infrastructure makes the landscape available and accessible. Making local vacations within Luxembourg more attractive reduces the number of trips and flights abroad, so the investment in fossil fuels can be reduced. But the strategy also aims to improve the micro economic system. Regional jobs can be created by promoting leisure tourism and local leisure activities. The awareness of natural resources and nature is increased through economic relevance and there is greater commitment to the preservation of natural space. And finally, improving the food, tourism, and cycling infrastructure in a sustainable way increases quality of life. Encouraging the use of local public transport and active mobility improves overall mobility in the region. More active mobility and alternative forms of mobility combined with a focus on regionality create a place that people want to both travel to and live in. The old railway line could be used to lead through the landscape and invite tourists to experience the delicacies of the region. This would create more appreciation for primary agricultural production, and small businesses would be preserved. In the long term, this would enable healthy production.

Fig. 174: Strategy for regional organic agriculture combined with culinary tourism (Decreasing global imports and avoiding CO^2 emissions through environmentally responsible land management)

Resources

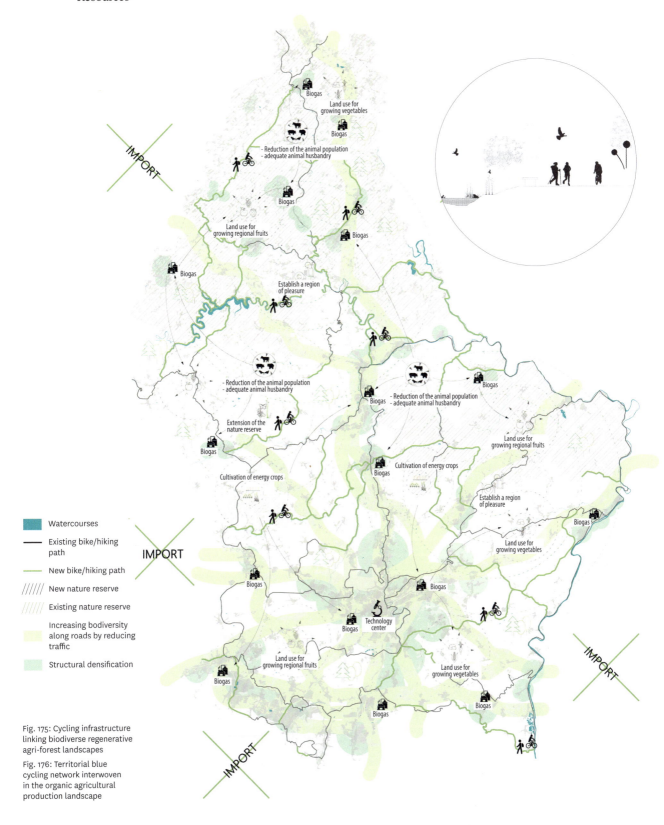

Fig. 175: Cycling infrastructure linking biodiverse regenerative agri-forest landscapes

Fig. 176: Territorial blue cycling network interwoven in the organic agricultural production landscape

Uncertainty

Disruptive innovations in technology and the economy but also climate catastrophes, hazards, health crises such as pandemics, or human caused disasters such as war can change spatial demands and necessities within weeks. This volatile dynamic asks for agile forms of planning and design, questioning traditional routines and practices. It offers moments of possibility to reflect on what is permanent and what can be changed. Acting instead of only reacting within invisible systems (high tech, CO_2 emissions, Covid-19 virus) might reveal the potential for dealing with these instabilities.

Transition means working in a mode of climate emergency and mobilizing all possible means. It offers the opportunity to develop not only resilient spatial solutions but even anti-fragile solutions in order to learn from the crisis. Transition is a situation of high uncertainty, doubt, and contradictions. It questions the velocity of dynamic urban or economic developments, advocating an immediate territorial transition but at the same time for slowness as a valuable asset for ecological regeneration.

Uncertainty

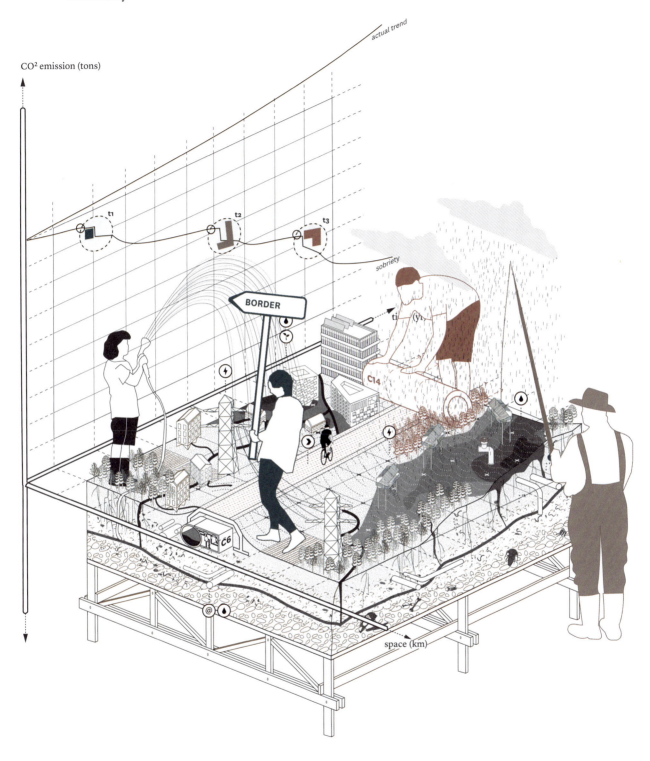

Fig. 177: Uncertainty and territory

Uncertainty

Urban acclimatization

Project details
Location: Luxembourg (LU)
Student: Myriam Oba

The Alzette winds close to the central station. Studying the networks reveals how a start could be made on a cogeneration development. The uses of the dense city are questioned, and the presence of nature in the city becomes an essential lever of understanding. The preliminary work on forests shows that there is an urgent need to try planting new species of trees and to acclimatize existing species to create adaptive ecosystems. Heat-producing networks in the city center have the potential to provide fertile land for use in creating a climatization territory (urban oasis). This could lead to the collaboration of living networks, forests, water networks, and sewers.

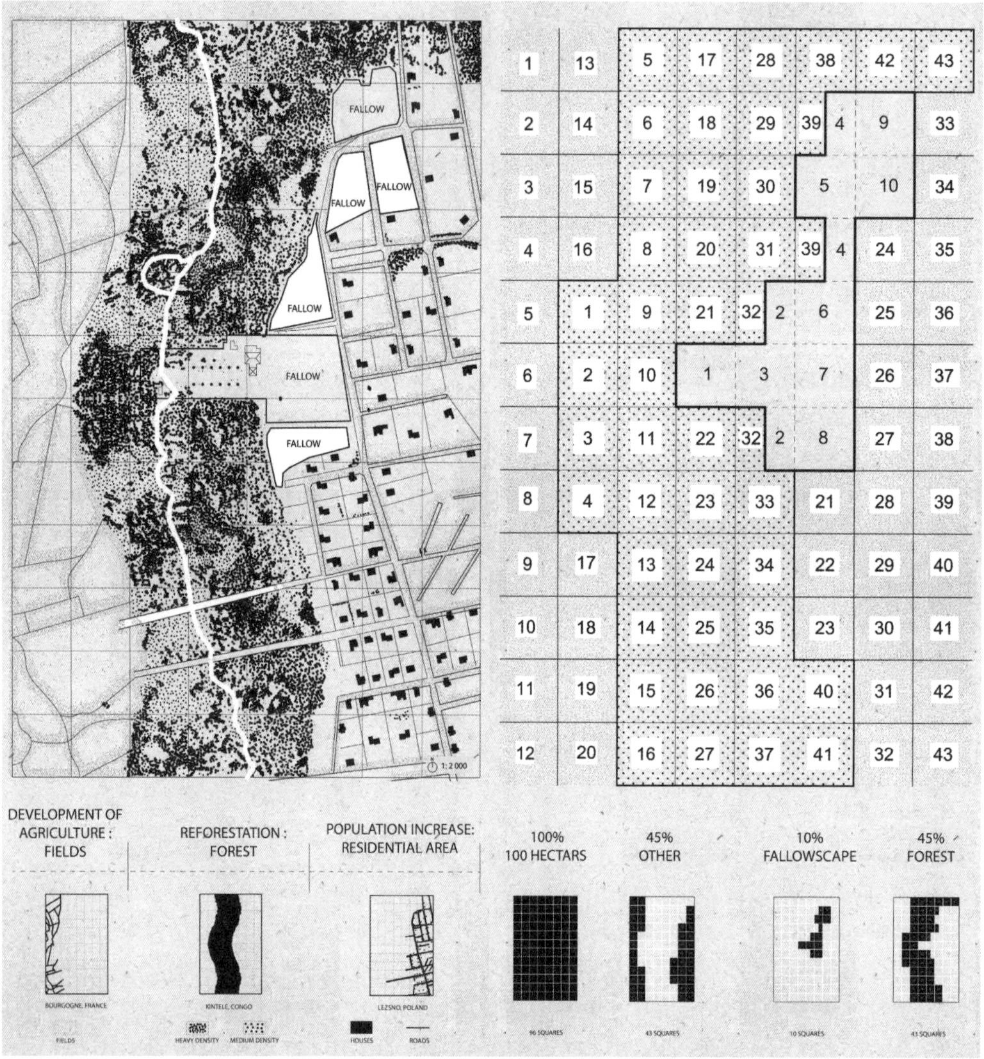

Fig. 178: Fallow land map
1/2 000

Fig. 179: Fallow land map
scheme 1/2 000

192

Uncertainty

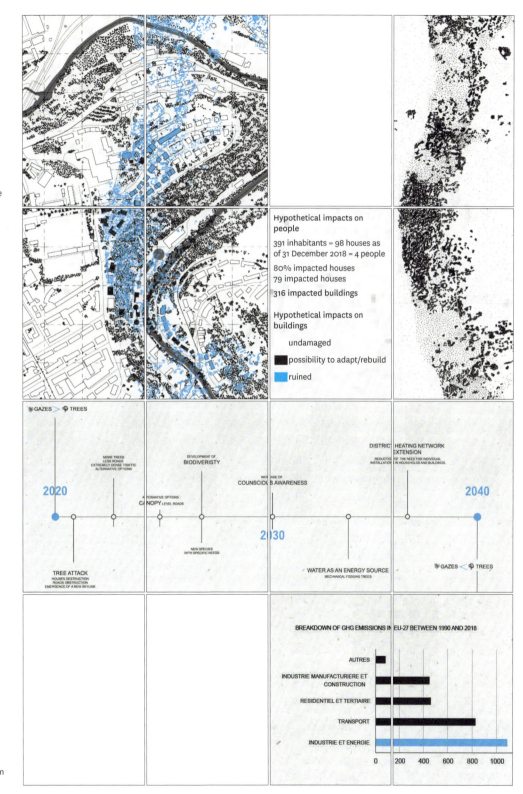

Fig. 180: Map of the forest attack 1/1 0000

Fig. 181: Current status of the forest 1/1 0000

Fig. 182: Quantity of impact

Fig. 183: Time of the forest attack

Fig. 184: Quantity of emission breakdown

More data—warm homes

Decentralized micro data center connecting Transit-Oriented Development (TODs) and fostering community life and active mobility in rural areas.

Challenge

The project addresses the territorial transition in relation to the process of digitalization. In a digital society digital infrastructure acquires an ever more central role. Luxembourg is one of the countries with the highest internet usage. Expansion of the fiberoptic network is still slow across the EU despite demand for faster internet growing exponentially every year. In Luxembourg, over 60 percent of all households already have direct access to high-speed internet.

However, remote territories may be excluded (digital divide) as market forces and a lack of public infrastructure investment (for example, the expansion of fiber-optic infrastructure) lead to access and/or performance issues on attempting to use the internet. This results in socially undesirable outcomes.

Strategy

The aim is to create a fragmented and decentralized digital infrastructure, following multiple principles, such as reducing the need for motorized transport through "new work" and working from home options or fighting urban sprawl by increasing the density of settlements connected to the railway infrastructure by transit-oriented development (TOD), which also offers the opportunity for co-working offices.

In general, mobility needs can be reduced in the process of digital change, for example, due to software solutions that grew immensely in popularity during the Covid-19 crisis such as web conference tools and food delivery, to name just two. Town centers can be densified and activated by TOD developments clustering different IT-related services and local retail stores, thus fighting urban sprawl. The TODs can add value to the community by providing co-working spaces for remote working or education. Furthermore, a future of shared and climate-neutral transportation is developed.

Uncertainty

Project details
Student: Philipp Misterek

Fig. 185: Decentralized micro data center connecting Transit-Oriented Development (TODs)

Uncertainty

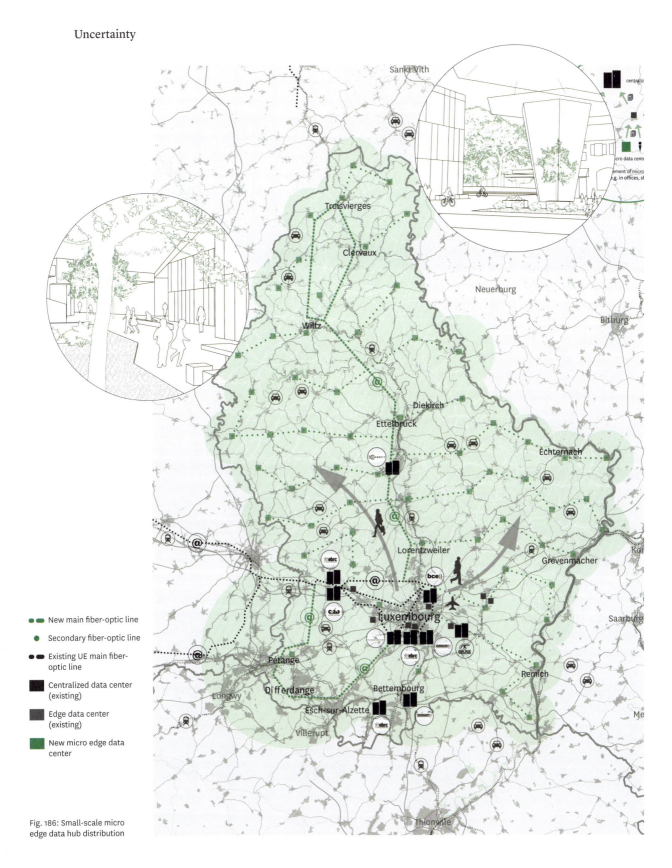

- ●● New main fiber-optic line
- ● Secondary fiber-optic line
- ●● Existing UE main fiber-optic line
- ■ Centralized data center (existing)
- ■ Edge data center (existing)
- ■ New micro edge data center

Fig. 186: Small-scale micro edge data hub distribution

IX.

Territorial Projects

Territorial projects in Europe are aiming to bring about structural, climatic, and eco-systemic transformations. They are to contribute to limiting global warming to a maximum of 1.5 degrees and in order to achieve this they need to propose, plan, and design profound changes spanning different borders and integrating different resources. This transition, combined with the enormous value of eco-systems, offers the chance to tackle global challenges such as climate change, species extinction, or renewable energy production on a territorial scale while at the same time embracing the uncertainties that come with these challenges.

This chapter presents six territorial projects and processes, showing an approach to addressing the territorial transition speculatively, in an experimental way. Summarizing these projects, this section not only explains the consultation with its aims, actors involved, and process but also presents examples of specific strategic territorial approaches as answers to the brief. The proposals from the interdisciplinary international teams offer inspiration for all design-related disciplines aiming to tackle the *wicked problem* of the territorial transition towards carbon-neutrality.

———

Luxembourg in transition

———

Rheinisches Revier

———

Greater Geneva

———

T.OP Noordrand

———

Raumbilder Lausitz

———

Amiter Tours

Territorial Projects

Luxembourg in Transition

Team participants

Paysage capital
AREP Ville SAS with Sorbonne Université, TAKTYK Sàrl, Mobil'homme Sàrl, QUATTROLIBRI EURL

Beyond Lux(e)!
MVRDV B.V. with Goudappel Coffeng, Transsolar Inc., H+N+S B.V., Deltares, DRIFT B.V., University of Twente, ITC Faculty

A guide to repairing a broken territory
Université du Luxembourg with LIST (Luxembourg Institute of Science and Technology), CELL (Centre for Ecological Learning Luxembourg), IBLA (Institut fir Biologësch Landwirtschaft an Agrarkultur asbl), OLM (Office for Landscape Morphology Co. Ltd)

Soil & people
2001 Sàrl with 51N4E bvba, LOLA, Systematica, Transsolar SAS, Endeavours, ETH Zurich, TU Kaiserslautern, Yellow Ball, Gregor Waltersdorfer, Maxime Delvaux, Office for Cities

Growing beyond borders & closing the loop
KCAP Architects&Planners GmbH with Arup Deutschland GmbH, Cabane Partner, Urbane Strategien und Entwicklung GmbH

Infrastructure Biorégionales Matiere, Circuits, Coalitions
TVK architecte et urbaniste Sàrl with Partie Prenante SASU, Soline Nivet Architecture SASU, Université Gustave Eiffel, laboratoire SPLOTT, SOL & CO, Justinien Tribillon, Université Grenoble Alpes, Institut de Géographie Alpine, Institut National de l'Économie Circulaire, Ecole nationale supérieure d'architecture de Nancy & laboratoire LhaC

Energyscapes
Raum404 GmbH with Topos, BASE paysage Sàrl, Basler & Hofmann West AG, Drees & Sommer GmbH, Novascopia Sàrl

MÉTABOLISER LES INVISIBLES, Nouvelles équations territoriales pour le Luxembourg
AWP Agence de reconfiguration territoriale with ONE Architecture, Arcadis, TU Delft, Harvard University GSD, Department of Landscape Architecture, Graz University of Technology, Institute for Urban Development, ITAR, École nationale supérieure d'architecture de Versailles

Luxeurope 2050 : Le grand-duché en transition
Interland Sàrl with Carbone 4 SAS, Auxilia asbl, ESAJ, École d'enseignement supérieur de paysage

Une vision pour le Luxembourg – Europe, terre
Studio Paola Viganò with EPF Lausanne, Habitat Research Center UCL, Université Catholique de Louvain, Metabolism of Cities, IDEA Strategische & Economisch Consulting NV, Serge Ecker

Luxembourg in Transition consultation platform
https://luxembourgintransition.lu

Luxembourg in Transition's team proposal reports
https://luxembourgintransition.lu/en/teams/

Territorial Projects

Ambition

International and interdisciplinary, the Consultation *Luxembourg in Transition* aims to gather elements of knowledge and strategic proposals for the development of the territory, and to produce ecological transition scenarios for the Grand Duchy of Luxembourg and the neighbouring border territories (the Luxembourg functional territory) up to 2050. Since this is one of the highest CO_2 emission countries per capita, the consultation required the investigation of processes that simultaneously increase the resiliency of the territory while also achieving a consensus of approval among the inhabitants. Conscious of the inter-boundaries' effects of the transition process, the consultation demanded to identify the Luxembourg functional area as scale of reference, with the purpose to comprehend the cross-national interventions over the following years.

Process

A restricted number of multidisciplinary teams have participated in a three-stage process to develop ecological transition scenarios. The teams selected at each stage were invited to deepen the research and visions of the previous phase, and simultaneously to develop innovative and effective tools, methods and

devices, thanks to an intense inter-disciplinary work with actors located within the territory of Luxembourg. The interim and final reports were entrusted to the Scientific Committee for detailed evaluation, which was accompanied by the opinion of the Inter-ministerial Committee and the Advisory Committee.

Actors

The consultation was organized by the Department of Spatial Planning of the Ministry of Energy and Spatial Planning, and it was monitored by three organs: the Inter-ministerial Committee, the Advisory Committee and the Scientific Committee, which are advisory and support bodies. In addition to these three bodies, a Citizens' Committee was structured to participate at the oral presentations of the consultation.

Text based on the project report "Soil & people" by 2001 S.rl with 51N4E bvba, LOLA, Systematica, Transsolar SAS, Endeavours, ETH Zurich TU Kaiserslautern, Yellow Ball, Gregor Waltersdorfer, Maxime Delvaux, Office for Cities

Territorial Projects

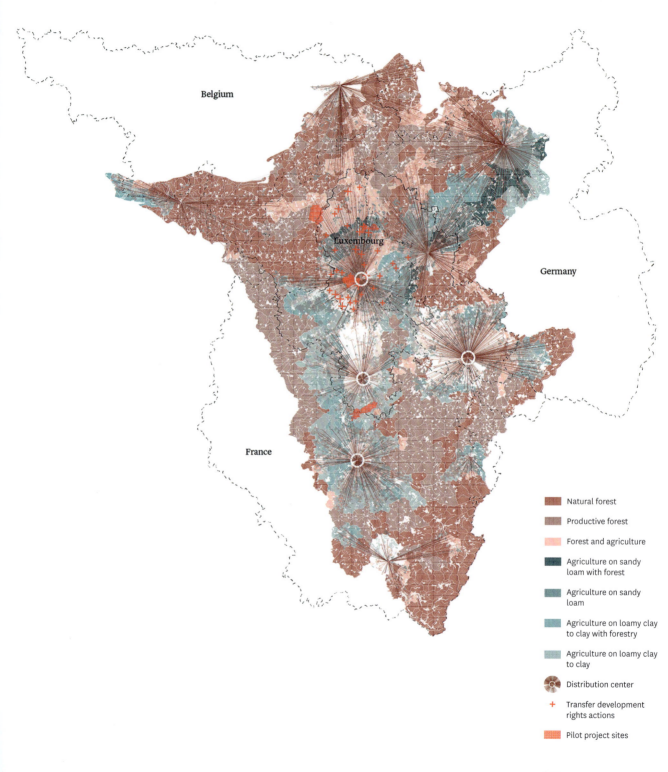

Territorial Projects

In the context of the participants outcomes, we propose an illustration made by superposition of the maps produced by the team Soil & People.[1]

A particular focus should be made here on the selected drawings in the following areas:
- the map related to agriculture production and the transportation system serving it[2]
- the land use map [3]
- the site interventions map [4]

These maps raise several questions, firstly: how can territories be defined when they are not congruent with political boundaries?

The team answered with a bio-functional region of Luxembourg greatly exceeding its political boundary and including parts of Germany, France and Belgium. The functional area expresses the need of interplay among nations in the path toward interrelated decarbonization processes.

Secondly, the maps question the scale of reference, and automatically by doing so the scale of intervention for the territorial decarbonization process? The outcome highlights the need for a multiscale approach and investigation, from the territorial level to the local one. Indeed, the interventions compose a constellation of local projects that strongly address the problematic of soil usage and impermeabilization.
In addition, the project areas are located in strategic areas of the functional area.

The territorial strategies have been showcased over two sites to articulate how such a vision can be implemented with concrete actions. These showcased applications are not absolute, but offer a recommended possibility. They can be further developed and altered to match better the contextual needs and ambitions.[5]

1 Project team: 2001 Sàrl (Luxembourg), 51N4E bvba (Belgium), LOLA (Netherlands), Systematica (Italy), Transsolar SAS (France), Endeavours (Belgium), ETH Zurich (Switzerland), TU Kaiserslautern (Germany), Yellow Ball (Luxembourg), Gregor Waltersdorfer (Luxembourg), Maxime Delvaux (Belgium), Office for Cities (France).

2 "Soil and people", Luxembourgintransition. Lu, 2022. pp. 116. Available at: https://luxembourgintransition.lu/wp-content/uploads/2021/06/2phase_2001-komprimiert.pdf. (Accessed 25 August 2022)

3 Ibid., pp. 121

4 Ibid., pp. 62

5 Ibid.

Project team: 2001 S.rl with 51N4E bvba, LOLA, Systematica, Transsolar SAS, Endeavours, ETH Zurich, TU Kaiserslautern, Yellow Ball, Gregor Waltersdorfer, Maxime Delvaux, Office for Cities

Fig. 187: Superimposition of analysis maps focused on agriculture, together with its related transport systems and distribution centers. The map highlights the bio-functional regions in Luxembourg and also experimental zones, which have the aim of establishing actions to transfer development rights for densification purposes.

Territorial Projects

Rheinisches Revier

Team participants

SEEN-REVIER 2.0
Albert-Speer & Partner

NetzRevier Gemeinsam Zukunft denken
ASTOC with urbanista.ch, LOLA Landscape Architects, mrs partner ag, FuturA

2 Millionen Morgen Land
yellow Z with ARGUS studio, berchtoldkrass, rabe landschaften, Dr. Stefan Carsten

Rheinisches Revier consultation
https://www.raum-strategie.de/

Ambition

The ambition for the Rhenish mining region is to become a competitive, high-performance region characterized by renewable energies, resource efficiency, and resource-saving consumption. The Rhenish Mining Region is transitioning towards becoming one of the first largely climate-neutral territories in Europe. Here, the creation of multi-coded landscapes—the combination of multiple functions such as photovoltaics, agricultural production, and the use of open spaces on the same surface—is important to solve the strong rivalry around land use. With this approach the territory might become more robust in the dynamic process of transition with ecological uncertainties of the coal exit.

Process

The "Spatial Strategy for the Rhenish Mining Region 2038+" (*Rheinisches Revier*) maps out a large-scale future direction for the territorial transition of the region. The spatial strategy is an informal development process in which the space is ambitiously developed, based on an economic structural program. In phase 1 planning, concepts, and inventories were collected. After that, in phase 2, three interdisciplinary planning teams were chosen in a tendering process and worked on a concept for the planning territory. In phase 3 the best approaches of the different thematic competencies are now being brought together in an integrated spatial strategy 2038+ 1.0 which will then be iteratively developed and revised.

Actors

The process of the strategy serves as a platform for regional actors with the aim of defining objectives together. The intensive participation process was designed with a steering group, a steering group +, municipal representatives, initiatives, and associations. Furthermore, the Mayors' Academy was established, which essentially served to communicate the expectations of the 53 different municipalities.

Text based on the project report "2 Millionen Morgen Land" by yellow Z with ARGUS studio, berchtoldkrass, rabe landschaften, Dr. Stefan Carsten and interview with Christa Reicher (Reicher Haase Assoziierte/RWTH Aachen)

Territorial Projects

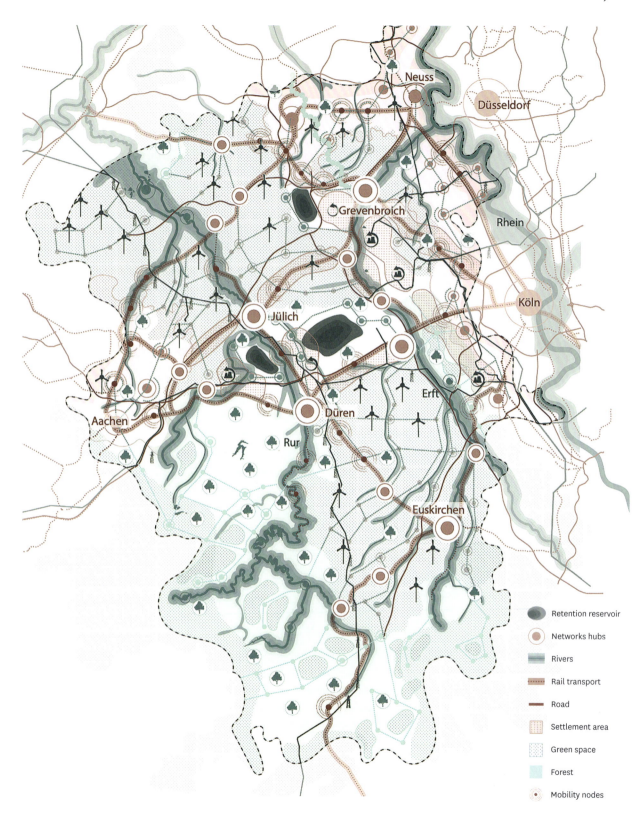

206

Territorial Projects

The soil is no longer the determinant for economic growth and prosperity, but it must be used frugally to meet the demands of climate change, agriculture, energy, nature and recreation. As soil is not multipliable, multi-coding (overlaying of multiple functions on the same area of soil) becomes the decisive large-scale design premise for the Revier. Roads are also multi-coded. They are not only designed for all transport modes but are also used for energy production and serve as biodiversity habitat corridors. A new verticality and mix are proposed that value and protect the resource of soil. Different territorial laboratories are proposed as test fields for speculative approaches with uncertain outcome in the process of transition. The soil in agricultural laboratories is not used only for food production. It is experimentally multi-coded for biodiverse climate protection with agri-food production such as agroforestry, meadow parks, species-rich agro-parks, heat-resilient farmland, or a CO_2-neutral agricultural park.

In water laboratories solutions are tested for water storage in periods of drought, for water retention and flood protection in the case of extreme rainfall events as well as drinking water management. They reclaim floodplain landscapes and ensure the re-wetting of swamps.

Locations and habitats throughout the territory are linked to each other by "multi-routes," which serve simultaneously as blue-green and mobility infrastructures, such as green urban-rural routes and water storage moats. Water and vegetation provide cooling while shrubs, hedges, and alleys offer protection from erosion and wind.

Project team: yellow Z with ARGUS studio, berchtoldkrass, Rabe Landschaften, Dr. Stefan Carsten

Fig. 188: Territorial landscapes are multi-coded as "multi-talents": These dense hybrids serve nature conservation, climate protection, agriculture, energy production, building land, and infrastructure without creating conflicts. The following concepts structure the proposal: Multi-coding of the landscape, multi-routes as mobility and species corridors, internal densification or densification along high-performance infrastructures, and expansion of existing tracks for logistics and public transport.

Territorial Projects

Greater Geneva

Team participants

Greater Geneva and its soil. Property, ecology, identity
ETHZ DARCH with Université du Luxembourg, Raumbureau

The great crossing: in search of singular ecologies
Interland with Bazar Urbain, Contrepoint, Coloco, Coopérative Équilibre, Lyon Urban School

Metabolizing the invisible
AWP (Agence de reconfiguration territoriale) with Topotek 1, Laboratory Alice-EPFL

Energy landscape
Raum404 with Lorenz Eugster Landscape architecture and urbanism, Università della Svizzera italiana, Emch+Berger, Thiébaut Parent – Drees & Sommer, Urban Studies – University of Basel

Resource regions
Apaar with Sofies, 6-t mobilité, Team Academy HES-SO, Irene Gil

On soil and work: The transition, a new biopolitical project
Habitat Research Center – EPFL with HEPIA, University of Neuchâtel, Product Life Institute

Geneva: metropolitan constellation
Stefano Boeri Architetti with Michel Desvigne Paysagiste, Baukuh, Transsolar Klima-Engineering, Systematica, DAStU Politecnico di Milano

Braillard Foundation
https://braillard.ch/?lang=en

Geneve 2050 consultation platform
https://braillard.ch/consultation-greater-geneva/?lang=en

Ambition

The investigation focused attention on possible paths that could leave Geneva as a resilient territory in a scenario of extreme effects caused by global warming.

Furthermore, since the exploratory work this involved was carried out in the course of the first pandemic wave, the state of art in respect to pandemic resilience that the Geneva urban area achieved has played a crucial role for the various propositions that were put forward. On the other hand, the proposed scenarios for Geneva have considered the practicable ways that will lead to a reduction of resource consumption in the pursuit of an improved environmental impact. The propositions explored have undoubtedly put forward innovative approaches that would reconfigure Geneva as either a zero-carbon, or negative a carbon urban area by using both resilient strategies and changes of habits in its inhabitants. In a nutshell, the competition had the clear intention of exploring the present and future role of Geneva in the global sphere of cities and regions committed to becoming carbon-free urban areas.

Process

A total of seven teams from different European backgrounds have had the opportunity to develop an innovative proposal for the territory. The two years consultation was structured in two stage dialogue moments, and in a series of exchange and discussions between teams and the consultations body.

Actors

The planning laboratory was organized and founded by Braillard Architects Foundation. Several actors worked in partnership for the competition with these ranging from la Fédération des Architects Suisse's (FAS) to the department of Haute-Savoie. On the other hand, the consultation body was composed of a wide participant spectrum with its figures composed of urbanists, architects, geographers and philosophers. The interdisciplinarity was seen as essential for critically evaluating each of the territorial proposals.

Text based on the project report "On soil and work: The transition, a new biopolitical project" by Habitat Research Center – EPFL with HEPIA, University of Neuch.tel, Product Life Institute

Territorial Projects

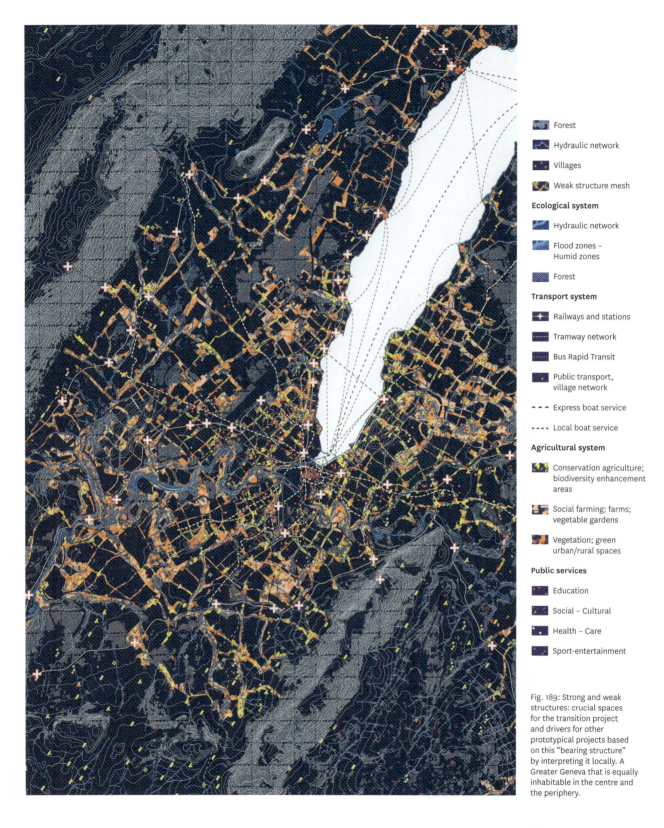

Forest
Hydraulic network
Villages
Weak structure mesh

Ecological system

Hydraulic network
Flood zones – Humid zones
Forest

Transport system

Railways and stations
Tramway network
Bus Rapid Transit
Public transport, village network
- - - Express boat service
---- Local boat service

Agricultural system

Conservation agriculture; biodiversity enhancement areas
Social farming; farms; vegetable gardens
Vegetation; green urban/rural spaces

Public services

Education
Social – Cultural
Health – Care
Sport-entertainment

Fig. 189: Strong and weak structures: crucial spaces for the transition project and drivers for other prototypical projects based on this "bearing structure" by interpreting it locally. A Greater Geneva that is equally inhabitable in the centre and the periphery.

The map of the previous page illustrates the proposition of the vision "Du sol et du travail. La transition, un nouveau projet biopolitique".[1]

The vision envisages a process that is both reformist and radical, and which is starting from the existing. Starting from the identification of the "weak structures", whose involve categories which have been marginalized in cities, such as water, soil regeneration, biodiversity, decentralized social and solidarity economy. The collective nature of this space represents a real 'special zone' of the transition project, and it is at the center of the team vision. These structures are considered as a space of continuity that guarantees the functions of ecosystems, as well as an opportunity for collective experimentation of innovative practices of the common space. New productive, social and solidarity-based processes are arranged in relation to weak structure, becoming levers for the requalification of the 'peripheries' of *Greater Geneva*. The proposed prototypical spaces, whose weak structure is the most strategic, show the various ways in which land and work are combined through activities that create value, whether ecological, economic or social.

The "weak structures" accompany the traditional "strong structures" and compose a habitable and territory, which is composed by a variety of urban and landscape forms. These supports are envisaged by the team as an opportunity to rethink the spatial and political project of *Greater Geneva*, a project of decentralization, territorial equilibrium and horizontal relations beyond the center and the periphery.

Project team: Centre de recherche Habitat – EPFL, Pr Paola Viganò (HRC director Lab-U), Pr Vincent Kaufmann (HRC-LASUR), Pr Alexandre Buttler (HRC-ECOS), MER. Luca Pattaroni (HRC-LASUR), Ass. Pr Corentin Fivet (HRC-SXL), Dr Roberto Sega (HRC – Lab-U, team coordinator), Tommaso Pietropolli (Lab-U, team co-coordinator), Dr Martina Barcelloni Corte (HRC – Lab-U), Dr Qinyi Zhang (HRC – Lab-U) with: Pr Pascal Boivin (inTNE-HEPIA, HES-SO),P Olivier Crevoisier (Université de Neuchâtel), Pr Walter R. Stahel (Product-Life Institute), Jonathan Normand (B Lab Switzerland), Isabel Claus, Ass. Pr Farzaneh Bahrami (Université de Groningen), Ass. Pr Chiara Cavalieri (Université Catholique de Louvain), Dr Thomas Guillaume, Dr Delphine Rime (Université de Berne), Eloy Llevat Soy (Politecnico di Torino), Marine Durand (LAB-U), Sylvie Nguyen (LAB-U) et Irène Desmarais, Simon Cerf-Carpentier, Noélie Lecoanet

Territorial Projects

T.OP Noordrand

Team participants

The Shared Valley
1010 Architeure and Urbanism with Sybrand Tjallingii, BOOM Landscapes, RR&AA, Ecores, Boom, Buck consultancy, Güller Güller

The European Boulevard
Artgineering with Idea Consult, Goudappel Coffeng, H+N+S Landscape architects.

Regionale visie op de Noordrand
Studio Bernardo Secchi Paola Viganò

T.OP Noordrand
www.topnoordrand.be

T.OP Noordrand, outcome workshop 1
www.slideshare.net/
RuimteVL/top-noordrand-
workshop1corijn

212

Territorial Projects

Ambition

T.OP Noordrand's "Territoriaal Ontwik-kelings Programma" is a spatial policy and not a conventional plan. It is a territorial vision linked to specific actions needed to realize the vision. It serves as a platform that brings together relevant stakeholders to develop a program of short- and medium-term realization based on common objectives. The objectives for the north border of Brussels (Noordrand) are: To accommodate demographical growth, to develop a sustainable mobility network, to strengthen open space, activate under-utilized space, and transition disruptive infrastructures, such as the Ring Road and the airport.

Actors

T.OP Noordrand is a multi-scale project by the Department of the Environment Flanders, Perspective Brussels, the province of Flemish Brabant, and the Flanders Public Waste Agency. It involves the minis-ters responsible for planning but also the various administration depart-ments. In the process, further coop-eration was established with private interested parties. The Noordrand program has integrated different resources and agents, such as current or planned sites and projects with strong co-creation ambition to give shape to a private and public cooper-ation. The aim is to create added value and develop synergies between the projects and the territorial vision.

Process

A first action program was created in 2016 and, during 2017, it was updated in an iterative, two-phase process which included the two Belgian regions (Brussels and Flanders) and three planning offices looking at three different segments of the territory. The experimental search, by trial and error, puts forward a development vision with stakeholders and, at the same time, clarifies the competences of the different regions and adminis-trative levels.

Text based on the project report "Airport Boulevard" by Artgineering with Idea Consult, Goudappel Coffeng, H+N+S Landscape architects and interview with Jan Zaman (Idea consult)

Territorial Projects

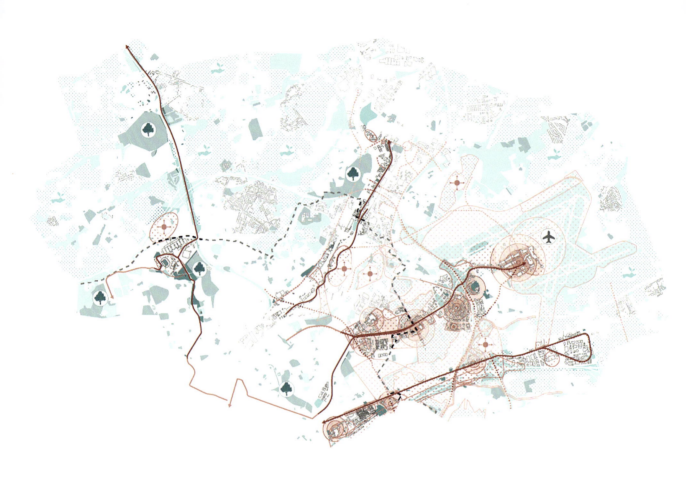

Territorial Projects

The transformation of a very dynamic territory, with a complex spatial reality and a multitude of private and public actors requires a method for identifying, conserving, and strengthening intrinsic qualities. The territory is heterogeneous and administratively complex, thus needing to remain a dynamic area. As an alternative to a top-down master plan, the strategy relies on concrete projects that are combined in manageable and well-communicable spatial and programmatic entities. It formulates scenarios that are sufficiently concrete and concise to enthuse the actors and encourage them to look beyond their own interests.

The transition aims at the reduction of the ecological footprint, improvement of the spatial function mix, a more resource-efficient urban metabolism, reduction of health risks (stricter standards apply to air quality, noise pollution, and soil quality), and a better living environment, with an emphasis on a multilingual and diverse population.

These targets are translated into three concrete scenarios concerning mobility, ecology, and education:

Mobility: A multimodal "European boulevard" from the Gare du Midi to the airport

Ecology: "Parc du Nord" is a structure of green and open spaces with agricultural, recreational, and functional connections

Education: The "NoordR'nD" transforms the mono-functional business district by turning offices into an educational institution.

The aim is to create added value and develop synergies between projects that have before often been carried out in isolation and to connect them to a platform. Part of the study incorporated how new projects or actions can be integrated and how links to possible stakeholders of these projects or actions can be created to reinforce the scenarios ("backcasting"). The project representatives and the different actors become the key players in the scenarios. Through the collaboration of the different actors, domino effects are created, which strengthen the individual projects and the territory as a whole.

Project team: Artgineering with Idea Consult, Goudappel Coffeng, H+N+S Landscape architects.

Fig. 190: System-related transition corridors towards reduction of ecological footprint and CO_2

Territorial Projects

Raumbilder Lausitz

Team participants

Bunter Bund Lausitz 2050
Berchtoldkrass space&options with Bauchplan, KONTEXTPLAN

Zeit für die Lausitz
CITYFÖRSTER with Freiwurf Landschaftsarchitekturen, Buro Happold, Thomas Gfeller

Lausitz 2025 Prolog einer Hyper Campus Region
KH STUDIO with GGR-Planung, Prof. Dr. Klaus Kunzmann, Egerer-Lab, Texturban – Rainer Müller

Die Lausitz wird WOWsitz!
Urban Catalyst with Brethdelacalle Architekten, Studio Amore

Lausitz transformation
https://transformation-lausitz.ioer.eu/fileadmin/user_upload/transformation-lausitz/files/raumlabor_dokumente/012022_ergebnisse_raumbilder_lausitz.pdf

Leibniz Institute of ecological urban and rural development (IOER)
https://www.ioer.de/

Ambition

The planning laboratory pursues two broad goals. Firstly, to create sustainable development perspectives for Lusatia through both the discourse during the process and the creation of a territorial vision. The aim is to contribute to the development of Lusatia, which is to be resilient, sustainable, and resource-conserving in its approach. The laboratory offers perspectives of ecological transition at different scales, considering normative orientation frameworks that aim to achieve the 1.5 degree target and take into account ecological challenges (e.g. European Green Deal, German sustainability strategy).

Secondly, the planning laboratory is to strengthen spatial planning in the process of structural transition by putting together spatially sensitive development strategies and connecting planning actors and regional governance structures in a cross-border cooperation, acting as a regional exchange platform.

Process

Four interdisciplinary teams were selected from a total of 24 teams participating in a public competition. They were commissioned in a non-anonymous, cooperative design process. The cooperative planning laboratory made the exchange between the planning teams and experts possible. Three colloquia (kick-off, intermediate, and final colloquia) as well as an excursion enabled professional and productive discussions.

Actors

The planning laboratory was organized by the Leibniz Institute for Ecological Spatial Development/Interdisciplinary Centre for Transformative Urban Redevelopment (IÖR/IZS) and was funded by the Federal Ministry of Education and Research. Together with KARO* architekten, the IÖR/IZS structured and implemented the laboratory while also undertaking additional scientific research on relevant topics. The advisory board consisted of diverse actors with local experience in research and practice, structural development, policy, and spatial science research from the regional universities.

Text based on the project report "Bunter Bund Lausitz 2050" and interview with Antje Heuer (Karo Architekten) and Jessica Theuner (IÖR/IZS)

Territorial Projects

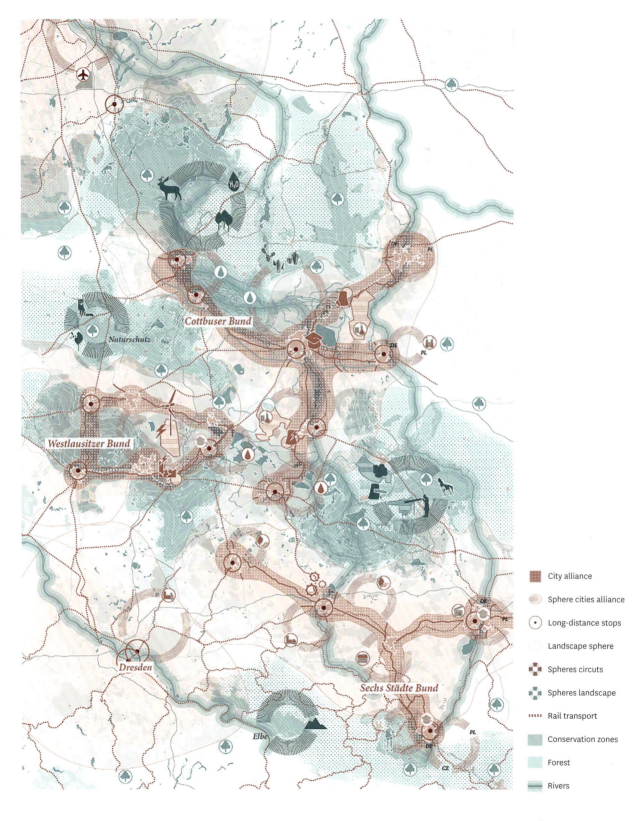

218

Three urban clusters are closely integrated into the territory and structure the spatial vision for the transition. These clusters create symbioses with large nature reserves and eco-systems. Small-scale, local material and climatic circular processes between city, hinterland, and nature are key for the territorial transition of Lusatia.

In contrast to the anthropocentric spaces in the region, large-scale physio-centric natural spaces flourish as dense wilderness that extends beyond ecological succession. These regenerative eco-systems can provide answers to challenges, such as fostering biodiversity and giving space to more-than-human agents through intensive forestation. The soils and moors naturally store CO_2 while the blue-green corridors with their water resources and green areas are the basis of a climate reserve for Lusatia with global importance. Common goods in the region such as supra-regional ecosystems or supra-regional infrastructures form a common regional identity. The "succeeding landscapes" are conceptualized as plural-possibility spaces in the face of uncertainties. Obsolete open-cast mining areas could be left to themselves, so that the groundwater can wash out the minerals from the soil and pioneer vegetation could reclaim the area. They could be actively transformed into wetlands so that the CO_2 reservoir could make Lusatia the global market leader for CO_2 certificates. Or the water pumps could stay in operation permanently and energy production (wind, solar, and hydro-electric power) could occupy the area, making Lusatia a strong energy region. Moreover, obsolete power plant sites can be important reserves for the unknown of tomorrow.

The hidden potential of the Lusatia region lies in taking advantage of the "landscape capacity" and its linkage with local value chains.

Project team: Berchtoldkrass space&options with Bauchplan, KONTEXTPLAN

Fig. 191: The principles of city alliances, spheres, succession landscapes, and wildernesses structure the transition.

Territorial Projects

Amiter Tours

Team participants

Project A
AWP (Agence de reconfiguration territoriale) with ZEFCO, Denis Brochard

Project B
CBA Blanchet Sarl with TAKTYK

Project C
Choreme with Denerier Martzolf Partenaires, Iaosenn

Project D
Agence Germe & Jam with Ma-Geo

Project E
Atelier Jean Chevalier with Rosalie Robert, Florent Delbreil, Belvédère, Prolog Ingénierie

Project F
Brigitte Philippon with Jean Kalt, Alain Gourdon, URBAN WATER

Project G
POLAU with Pratiques Urbaines, Bruno Marmiroli

Project H
Sophie Blanc Atelier d'architecture with Benjamin Breton, Maxime Caillon, ARP-Astrance, Théo Dubrul, Eva Feuillard, Raphaël Gubler, Karim Lahiani, Sylvain Rode, Mathieu Serreau, Chris Younes

French ministry for the ecological transition

https://www.ecologie.gouv.fr/programme-Amiter-concours

PUCA (Plan Urbanisme Costruction Architecture)

http://www.urbanisme-puca.gouv.fr/concours-amiter-mieux-amenager-les-territoires-en-a2213.html

Territorial Projects

Ambition

The consultation was created with the intention to investigate approaches and solutions able to deal with the increasing number of extreme events caused by the raising global temperature in France. In fact, the episodes span from forests fire in the South of France to violent floods in the Center and the North, with the natural disaster cost expected to rise by 50% over thirty years. Pursuing this purpose, the AMITER competition was conceived to investigate:
- urban reconfigurations able to generate resilient environments against critical climate events;
- the use of risks as a source of innovation, and especially as a resource for human activities;
- the possible paths of adaptations through the collaboration of experts coming from a wide spectrum of discipline.

Actors

The consultation was organized by PUCA (Plan Urbanisme Construction Architecture) under the lead of the French Ministry for Ecological Transition, while each site has been previously investigated by CEREMA (Study center for risks, environment, mobility and development), with the intention to provide qualitative information to the participants. Lastly, the jury has been composed by an interdisciplinary group of experts and a selected group of citizens for each site.

Process

Similarly to the Europan, the consultation started with a declaration of interest from local authorities to identify potential sites. Among the 43 proposed site only 9 were selected for the consultation. Secondly, it started the declaration of interest moment for architecture/urban teams, and between the 91 applicants only 71 have been accepted (8 per site).

Text based on the project report AWP with ZEFCO, Denis Brochard

Territorial Projects

222

Territorial Projects

In the strategy proposed by AWP for Tours, the issue is about risk management and compensation. The environmental compensatory aspect of the on-going urban development project here is underlined by the fact that it is actually located next door to the train station. In fact, the AWP planning focus could justifiably be seen as the fallow field of future development, an area characterized by slowness and ecological experimentation. The proposal thus raises the question of a possible integration for the experimental ecological area as an active compensatory element for future development.

In the risk management context, the proposal opens the dialogue about defining possible areas of planted, floodable surfaces, the economy of these and their phasing in order to establish a rhythm and a logic to welcoming water and to introduce fullness on the plot.

This is a strategy that reflects the possibility of welcoming risk and transforming it into a valuable resource, a resource capable of being transformed into a multitude of creative uses.

Project team: AWP (Agence de reconfiguration territoriale) with ZEFCO, Denis Brochard

Fig. 192: Guide plan of land use quantity facing multiple risks.

Appendix

Appendix

Biographies

Matthias Armengaud
is an architect, urbanist, and a founding member and director of the AWP office for territorial reconfiguration, an award-winning interdisciplinary design office, based in Paris. AWP develops international projects, working on a wide variety of programs such as a vision for *Greater Geneva*, a giant canopy in Norway, an Insect Museum near Paris, the transformation strategy for Paris la Defense CBD, the Lausanne west extension, *Luxembourg in transition*, or an international research program on cities at night (the Troll Protocol). Projects by AWP were nominated for the European Mies Van der Rohe Award in 2009, 2014, and 2017. Matthias Armengaud is a guest professor for the sustainable planning master's program at the École nationale supérieure d'architecture de Versailles and has taught project studios at the Berlage Institute at Delft University of Technology and the Harvard Graduate School of Design among others.

Marc Armengaud
is a tenured professor at Paris-Malaquais Architecture School, covering both projects and theory in his teaching. He studied philosophy at the Sorbonne, focusing on Maurice Merleau-Ponty and a transdisciplinary approach to phenomenology. Alongside researching and teaching, he was actively involved in writing hybrids of fiction and essays, and producing documentary-fictions for the French public radio program "France Culture," as well as being involved in the temporary occupation of the Palast der Republik in Berlin. Marc Armengaud is now co-directing the office AWP with his brother Matthias. He develops research

and experiment projects, and directs publications, films, and exhibitions. He curated the Paris la Nuit exhibition and authored its catalogue for the Pavillon de l'Arsenal in Paris in 2013, as well as curating the book and pavilion Vulnerability, how are we doing? for the Venice Biennale in 2021. He is an experienced lecturer and was recently guest critic at the Harvard Graduate School of Design.

Stefan Bendiks
is an architect and urban designer. In 2001, he founded Artgineering together with Aglaée Degros. He devises and implements design strategies for complex inter-urban conditions with a great interest in mobility and, in particular, in the potential of cycling to create a better city. In various research and design projects, he reinterprets the relation between mobility, landscape, and urban development. Stefan Bendiks has taught and lectured on architecture, urban planning, and design at various institutions such as Delft University of Technology, Graz University of Technology, Artez Arnhem, the Academy of Fine Arts in Vienna, the Politechnico Milano, and the Harvard Graduate School of Design. He advises several cities in Europe and further afield on their cycling strategy as a member of the Dutch Cycling Embassy. Bendiks is co-author of publications such as the inspirational handbook Cycle Infrastructure, the study Fietsland (Cycling Nation), commissioned by the Dutch Ministry of Infrastructure & Environment, and Traffic Space is Public Space.

Anita Berrizbeitia
is a professor of landscape architecture. Her research focuses on design theories of modern and contemporary landscape architecture, the productive aspects of landscapes, and Latin American cities and landscapes. She was awarded the 2005/2006 Prince Charitable Trusts Rome Prize Fellowship in Landscape Architecture. A native of Caracas, Venezuela, she studied architecture at the Universidad Simon Bolivar before receiving a BA from Wellesley College and an MLA from the Harvard Graduate School of Design.
Berrizbeitia has taught design theory and studios, most recently at the University of Pennsylvania School of Design, where she was associate chair of the Department of Landscape Architecture. Her studios investigate innovative approaches to the conceptualization of public space, especially on sites where urbanism, globalization, and local cultural conditions intersect. She also leads seminars that focus on significant transformations in landscape discourse over the last three decades. From 1987 to 1993 she practiced with Child Associates, Inc., in Boston, where she collaborated on many award-winning projects.

Matthijs Bouw
is a Dutch architect and urbanist, and founder of One Architecture and Urbanism, an award-winning Amsterdam- and New York-based design and planning firm that is a global leader in the use of design for climate adaptation and mitigation. He is professor of practice McHarg Center fellow for risk and resilience Penn. Bouw's work at Penn theorizes and

Appendix

positions design as an integrator and innovator among scales, disciplines, actors, and issues in urban resilience, water management, and energy transition projects. Additionally, he researches how to achieve and increase "resilience value" in the implementation of complex projects. At Weitzman, Bouw teaches the interdisciplinary seminars "Design with Risk" and "Public Health, Cities and the Climate Crisis," as well as the 'Urban Resilience Studio'. In 2000 Matthijs Bouw co-curated the Dutch Pavilion at the Venice Biennale together with Kristin Feireiss. In addition he has published articles and reviews in many architectural publications. Bouw's most recent book, Building with Nature focuses on nature-based solutions for climate change adaptation and mitigation.

Aglaée Degros
is professor and head of the Institute of Urbanism at Graz University of Technology and honorary science fellow at the Vrije Universiteit in Brussels. She was born in 1972 in Leuven in Belgium and studied architecture in Brussels, Karlsruhe, and Tampere. In 2001, together with Stefan Bendiks, she founded Artgineering. Degros has held various teaching positions and visiting professorships at Delft University of Technology, Rotterdam Academy of Architecture, the Vrije Universiteit in Brussels, the Academy of Fine Arts Vienna, Vienna University of Technology, the Politechnico Milano, and the Harvard Graduate School of Design, among others. Aglaée Degros is co-author of books such as the Routledge publication Public Space and the Challenges of Urban Transformation in Europe, Traffic Space is Public Space, Territorial Justice and, more recently, Basics of Urbanism. She is a regular jury member for international urban planning and design competitions.

Florian Dupont
is an urbanist with an environmental background. In 2018 he co-founded Zefco—an agency for environmental studies dedicated to the ecological transition. Dupont works on low-carbon targets in the urban realm with a special focus on rehabilitation and a broader awareness of the urgency of environmental crisis in society. He studied urbanism at Paris-Sorbonne University and at the Universidade NOVA de Lisboa as well as environmental and energy studies at the University of East London. He was associate lecturer at the Université Paris-Est-Marne-la-Vallée (UPEM) at the French Institute of Urban Planning. Later he was project manager and director, in charge of the City and Territories division at Franck Boutté Consultants from 2012 to 2018. He recently co-authored the report Transitions in the regime of controversies around the Lake of Grand-Lieu for the Ministry of Ecological Transition and Territorial Cohesion.

Simon Hartmann
is an architect and chair of building planning and design at the Department of Architecture at Karlsruhe Institute of Technology and visiting professor at the Harvard Graduate School of Design. He was born in 1974 in Bern, Switzerland, and studied architecture at the École polytechnique fédérale de Lausanne, Berlin University of Technology, and the Eidgenössische Technische Hochschule Zürich (ETH Zurich). In 2003, together with Tilo Herlach and Simon Frommenwiler, he founded HHF Architects. He received national and international awards with HHF, such as the Design Vanguard 2010 and the Wallpaper Design Award in 2012 , for which they were already nominated in 2010. HHF was awarded an American Architecture Award in 2009 and 2013. In 2013 HHF also won the German Houses of the Year award, and in 2014 they were awarded the Swiss Architecture Award. Hartmann has held various teaching positions and visiting professorships

at ETH Studio Basel, the Haute école d'ingénierie et d'architecture de Fribourg, the University of Innsbruck, Karlsruhe Institute of Technology, and Yale School of Architecture.

Panos Mantziaras
is an architect, engineer, and director of the Braillard Architectural Foundation. He received his PhD in urban design and planning from the Université Paris. He has published, lectured, and taught in Europe, North America, and Japan and is the author of La ville-paysage, Rudolf Schwarz et la dissolution des villes. As head of the Office for Architectural, Urban and Landscape Research at the French Ministry of Culture and Communication from 2011 to 2015, he initiated research programs on architecture and urbanism in the context of the ecological transition. As director of the Geneva-based Braillard Architectural Foundation since 2015, he launched the research and cultural program The Eco-Century Project®, which certified the international consultations for Greater Geneva and the cross-border region of Luxembourg. He recently co-published Dessiner la Transition, Dispositifs pour une métropole écologique and Racines modernes de la ville contemporaine.

Anna Positano
is a photographer and artist with a background in architecture. She studied at the University of Geneva and the London College of Communication. Her work addresses the relation between society and landscape in order to study everyday places that form the narration of people's lives. She uses a variety of formats such as photography, video, or installations to express the complexity of anthropocentric landscapes. In addition to her art and research, she works on commission for architects and public institutions. She is regularly published in architectural magazines including Casabella, Domus, L'Architecture d'aujourd'hui, and Le Moniteur. She gives lectures at

Appendix

the École Polytechnique Fédérale de Lausanne (EPFL), Florida International University, the Polytechnico Milano, and the University of Genoa, among others. Her projects have been exhibited internationally, in art galleries and public institutions, such as La Triennale, Milan, Venice Architectural Biennale, Cornell University, Ithaca, Ljubljana Museum of Architecture and Design, and Villa Croce Museum of Contemporary Art, Genoa.

Radostina Radulova-Stahmer

is an architect with a focus on urbanism and currently holds a postdoc position at the Institute of Urbanism at Graz University of Technology. She studied architecture at Karlsruhe Institute of Technology and at the Higher Technical School of Architecture of Madrid (ETSAM) and received her Diploma of Architecture with honors in 2010. In her PhD she researched the spatial effects of digital change in 2021 at Karlsruhe Institute of Technology and Graz University of Technology. From 2013-2017, she worked as a scientific associate (pre-doc) at the Institute of Design and Urban Planning at the Leibniz University Hannover. Prior to this she worked in several international offices. In 2010 she co-founded the office STUDIOD3R with Deniza Horländer, which received several international awards, such as 1st prize at Europan Graz in 2017 or 1st Prize at the Young Architects Program at MAXXI Rome in collaboration with MoMA and MoMA PS1 New York, and the Constructo Association of Santiago de Chile. Her research and work focus on climate-oriented urban design and urban transformation in the digital revolution. She is part of the scientific advisory board of the Wüstenrot Stiftung.

Eva Schwab

is a landscape architect, post-doctoral university assistant, and deputy head of the Institute of Urbanism at Graz University of Technology. Her work focuses on spatial and territorial justice in planning and design, both in urban and rural settings. She studied landscape architecture in Vienna and Barcelona. In 2015 she received her doctorate summa cum laude in landscape planning and landscape architecture from the University of Natural Resources and Life Sciences, Vienna. Her PhD was awarded the Landscape Research Dissertation Prize and published in 2018 as the monograph Spatial Justice and Informal Settlements: The Comunas of Medellín by Emerald. After her PhD, she worked as a post-doctoral researcher on public space issues in interdisciplinary teams at various universities, such as Vienna University of Technology, the University of Natural Resources and Life Sciences, Vienna, and Nürtingen-Geislingen University. She has published widely on public and green space in international books and journals.

Ingrid Taillandier

is an architect and teaches at the École nationale supérieure d'architecture de Versailles, where she is director of the Franco-Chinese double master's degree program in ecological urbanism run by the École nationale supérieure d'architecture de Versailles and Tongji University in Shanghai. She studied at Paris-Belleville School of Architecture and Columbia University in New York. Her focus is on urban planning in the context of climate risk, considering elements such as water and river banks in their transformation. She has been head of ITAR architectures since 2006 following earlier collaborations with Richard Meier and Behnish and partners. Taillandier writes for magazines such as AMC and TOPOS and her interest in density and high-rise buildings inspired her to write several articles on these specific topics and give lectures around the world.

Appendix

École nationale supérieure d'architecture de Versailles student list
Academic year 2020-2021

Alizée Bearzi: Metropolitan reconfigurations and transformation of network, Inaccessible Nature

Thomas Breton: On the edge of concentration, Insects

Suzanne Brigaud: Territories of cogeneration, Night River

Aymeric Brouez: Large technical systems and sliding, Marshes attack

Louise Ciceri: Hyper Nature, The Marshes

Gaelle Decheneaux: On the edge of concentration, The Water Plant

Pino Heye: Large technical systems and sliding, Immediate blocking

Soohye (Stella) Jeong: On the edge of concentration, Landscape re-connection

Cécile Kermaidic: On the edge of concentration, Animals are the keystone

Caitlin Lam Tze Ting: Metropolitan reconfigurations and transformation of network, Mutation Logitics

Ronan Le Cornec: Border/Strategic Cross-Border Sites, Trinational

Raquel Maio Pinto de Mesquita: Hyper Nature, Mining Heritage

Myriam Oba: Territories of cogeneration, Urban re-climatization

Loris Peziere: Hyper Nature, Weakened Nature

Rhita Adnane: Border/Strategic Cross-Border Sites, Groundwater

Micaela Sepulveda: Metropolitan reconfigurations and transformation of network, Industrial Area

Salila Sihou: Border/Strategic Cross-Border Sites, Transborder Archipelago

Maria Zboralska: Territories of cogeneration, Inner Border

Instructors

Matthias Armengaud

Ingrid Taillandier

assisted by: **Bérénice Gentil**

Guest lectures/jury

Marc Armengaud
Lecture on the "Prospective visions for *Greater Geneva*"

Anita Berrizbeitia

Matthijs Bouw

Aglaée Degros

Florian Dupont
Lecture on density and carbon emission

Simon Hartmann
Lecture on the house of revolution in Montenegro

Anna Positano

Andrea Bagnato
Together with Anna gave a lecture on the utopian city of "Arborea" in Sicilia

Appendix

Graz University of Technology student list
Academic year 2020-2021

Mendi Kocis
Office to go

Carina Mazelle
Fuel for life

Carola Hilgert
Caring loop

Marie-Theres Schwaighofer
Stay put

Beatrice Wagner
Gourmet region

Philipp Misterek
More data—warm homes

Gauthier Desplace
Cycling on that asset

Alexia Petra Eberl
Productive mix

Lara Patricia Thonhofer
Com(mix)ial

Instructors

Aglaée Degros

Radostina Radulova-Stahmer

Guest lectures/jury

Anita Berrizbeitia
Guest at mid-term crit and finals

Panos Mantziaras
Guest at mid-term crit and finals

Carole Schmit
Guest input

Matthias Armengaud
Guest at finals

Appendix

Acknowledgements

To Tadzio, Lou, Tilo and Koba

The book has been the outcome of the research, discussion, and opportunities that occurred over several years. We would like to express our sincere gratitude to the École nationale supérieure d'architecture de Versailles students of the course "P45 Invisible metropolis" and the students of the master studio "Luxembourg in Transition" from Graz University of Technology for the stimulus that they have brought in the field of territorial transition since 2017, as well as to our colleagues Augustin Cornet, Emilie Gascon, Florian Hertweck, and Laureline Guilpain. A special thanks goes to Jean Christophe Quinton, Emeric Lambert, Jeanne-Marie Portevin, Virginie David, Marie Hélène Amiot, and Paula Delprato for their engagement through the École nationale supérieure d'architecture de Versailles. We would also like to thank David Mangin, Jean Castex, Philippe Panerai, and Casimir Boccanfuso for the transmission of their knowledge and passion as teachers.

A special thanks goes to the Braillard Foundation for creating the occasion of the *Greater Geneva* consultation, a unique experience for developing ideas and visions, in collaboration with the EPFL laboratory ALICE, Topotek 1, Fondation AIA ville santé environnement, AIA environnement, Altostep, Bonnard et Gardel ingenieurs conseils, Jeanne Della Casa, Fas L-Architectes, Géraldine Pflieger, Université de Genève, Stefan Kaegi, Rimini Protokoll, Jean Delons, Vinci, Yann Moulier Boutang, Université de technologie de compiègne, Paul Schneeberger, Schweizer Städteverband, Mark Schneiter, and Schneiter Verkehrsplanung. Equally, our gratitude goes to the Government of the Grand Duchy of Luxembourg, Ministry of Energy and Spatial Planning Department for implementing the *Luxembourg in transition* consultation. We also very much valued the rare chance for developing and discussing ideas with Matthijs Bouw, ONE Architecture; Dirk Sijmons, Delft University of Technology; Anita Berrizbeitia, Harvard University GSD; Aglaée Degros, Graz University of Technology, Institute for Urbanism; Ingrid Taillandier, ITAR and Arcadis.

Furthermore, Sarah M. Whiting, Harvard University GSD, Gary R. Hilderbrand, Harvard University GSD, Petra Peterson, Graz University of Technology, Mohsen Mostafavi, Harvard University GSD, Barbara Herz, Graz University of Technology, Fondation Luma, and The Berlage University for Advanced Studies need a special acknowledgment for the opportunities for teaching and discussion they have offered over several years, which prompted unique moments of reflection that have produced many contributions for this publication.

Appendix

Further readings

Abalos, Iñaki. Campos De Batalla. Barcelona: Col·legi Oficial d'Arquitectes de Catalunya,2005.

Armengaud, Marc.Paris La Nuit: Chroniques Nocturnes: Paris, Pavillon De L'Arsenal, 23 Mai - 6 Octobre 2013. Paris: Picard, 2013.

Bachelard, Gaston. Le Droit De Rêver. Paris: Presses universitaires de France, 2013.

Bendiks, Stefan, and Aglaée Degros. Traffic Space Is Public Space. Zurich: Park Books, 2020.

Cavalieri, Chiara, and Viganò Paola. HM The Horizontal Metropolis: A Radical Project. Zurich, Switzerland: Park Books, 2019.

Cavalieri, Chiara, Paola Viganò, and Martina Barcelloni Corte. The Horizontal Metropolis. Between Urbanim and Urbanization . Springer, 2018.

Corte, Martina Barcelloni, and Viganò Paola. The Horizontal Metropolis: The Anthology. Cham, Switzerland: Springer, 2022.

Crary, Jonathan. 24/7: Late Capitalism and the Ends of Sleep. London: Verso, 2014, Degros, Aglaée, Anna Bagaric, Sabine Bauer, Radostina Radulova-Stahmer, Mario Stefan, and Eva Schwab. Basics of Urbanism: 12 Begriffe Der Territorialen Transformation = 12 Notions of Territorial Transformation. Zurich: Park Books, 2021.

De Geyter, Xaveer. After Sprawl: Research for the Contemporary City. Rotterdam: Nai, 2002. Desvigne, Michel, and Gilles A. Tiberghien. Jardins Elementaires. (ROME): Ed. Carte segrete, 1988.

Ferrari, Marco, Elisa Pasqual, and Andrea Bagnato. A Moving Border: Alpine Cartographies of Climate Change. New York, NY: Columbia Books on Architecture and the City, 2019.

Gemenne, François, and Aleksandar Rankovic. Atlas De L'anthropocène. Paris: Sciences Po Les Presses, 2021. Gethmann, Daniel, ed. Territorial Justice. GAM. Berlin: Jovis Verlag GmbH, 2019.

Gilpin, William, and Joël Cornuault. Le Paysage De La Forêt. Saint-Maurice (Val-de-Marne): Premières pierres, 2010.

Guattari, Félix. The Three Ecologies. London: Bloomsbury, 2014. Hache, Emilie, and Notéris Emilie. Reclaim: Anthologie De Textes écoféministes. Paris: Cambourakis, 2016.

Handke Peter, and Le Olivier Lay. Essai Sur Le Lieu Tranquille. Paris: Gallimard, 2014. Harrison, Robert Pogue, and Florence Naugrette. Forêts: Essai Sur L'imaginaire Occidental. Paris: Flammarion, 1992.

Hertweck, Florian, Sébastien Marot, O. M. Ungers, Rem Koolhaas, Peter Riemann, Hans Kollhoff, and Arthur Ovaska. The City in the City: Berlin: A Green Archipelago. Zurich: Lars Müller, 2013.

Hopkins, Rob. The Transition Handbook: From Oil Dependency to Local Resilience. Vermont: Chelsea Green publishing, 2008. Ingold, Tim. The Life of Lines. London: Routledge, 2015.

Kellogg, Scott T. Urban Ecosystem Justice: Strategies for Equitable Sustainability and Ecological Literacy in the City. Abingdon, Oxon: Routledge, Taylor & Francis Group, 2022.

Khosravi, Hamed, Taneha Kuzniecow Bacchin, and Filippo LaFleur. Aesthetics and Politics of Logistics: Venice, Rotterdam. Milan: Humboldt books, 2019.

Kleilein, Doris. Post-Pandemic Urbanism. Berlin: Jovis, 2021.

Latour, Bruno, and Catherine Porter. Facing Gaia: Eight Lectures on the New Climatic Regime. Cambridge: Polity Press, 2021.

Latour, Bruno, and Emilie Hermant. Paris Ville Invisible. Paris: Éditions B42, 2021.

Latour, Bruno, and Catherine Porter. Down to Earth: Politics in the New Climatic Regime. Cambridge: Polity Press, 2019.

Luque Gómez, Mariano, and Ghazal Jafari.

Posthuman. Cambridge, MA: New Geographies Lab, Harvard University Graduate School of Design, 2017.

Lynch, Kevin. What Time Is This Place? Cambridge, Mass: MIT Press, 2009. Malm, Andreas. White Skin, Black Fuel: On the Danger of Fossil Fascism. London: Verso, 2021.

Marot, Sebastien. Sub-Urbanism and the Art of Memory. S.l.: Architectural Association, 2022. Moretti, Franco, Étienne Dobenesque, and Laurent Jeanpierre. Graphes, Cartes Et Arbres: Modèles Abstraits Pour Une Autre Histoire De La Littérature. Paris: Les Prairies ordinaires, 2008.

Appendix

Munari, Bruno. Disegnare UN Albero. Mantova: Corraini, 2017. Munarin, Stefano, and Maria Chiara Tosi. Tracce Di Città: Esplorazioni Di Un Territorio Abitato: L'area Veneta. Milan: Angeli, 2002.

Pörtner, H.-O. Climate Change 2022: Impacts, Adaptation and Vulnerability. Geneva, Switzerland: WMO, IPCC Secretariat, 2022.

Raworth, Kate. Doughnut Economics: Seven Ways to Think like a 21st-Century Economist. London: Penguin, 2022.

Rettich, Stefan, and Sabine Tastel. Die Bodenfrage. Klima, Ökonomie, Gemeinwohl. Berlin: Jovis Verlag GmbH, 2020.

Steenbergen, Carsten. Atlas of the New Dutch Water Defence Line. Rotterdam: 010 Publ, 2007.

Stern, Mario Rigoni. Arbres En Liberté. Lyon: La fosse aux ours, 1998.

Dirk, Sijmons, Conny Bakker, Machiel van Dorst, and Douglas Heingartner. Landscape and Energy: Designing Transition. Rotterdam: Nai010 Publishers, 2014.

Texier, Simon. Voies Publiques: Histoires & Pratiques De L'espace Public à Paris: CET Ouvrage Est Publié à L'occasion De L'exposition ..., Mars 2006. Paris: Picard, 2006.

Too Blessed to Be Depressed: Crimson Architectural Historians 1994-2002. Rotterdam: 010 Publishers, 2002.

Varnelis, Kazys. The Infrastructural City: Networked Ecologies in Los Angeles. Barcelona: Actar, 2009.

Viganò, Paola, Lorenzo Fabian, and Bernardo Secchi. Water and Asphalt: The Project of Isotropy. Zurich: Park Books, 2016.

Yokoyama, Yūichi. Travaux Publics. Montreuil (Seine-Saint-Denis): Matière, 2010.

Zardini, Mirko, and Wolfgang Schivelbusch. Sense of the City: An Alternate Approach to Urbanism. Baden: Lars Müller Publishers, 2006.

Appendix

Bibliography

Armengaud, Marc, and Alexandre Labasse. Paris La Nuit: Chroniques Nocturnes: Exposition, Paris, Pavillon De L'Arsenal, 23 Mai – 6 Octobre 2013. Paris: Pavillon de l'Arsenal, 2013.

Armengaud, Marc, Matthias Armengaud, and Alessandra Cianchetta. Nightscapes: Paisajes Nocturnos = Nocturnal Landscapes. Barcelona: GG, 2009.

Bailly, Jean-Christophe. Le Dépaysement: Voyages En France. Paris: Seuil, 2011.

Banerji, Bibhouti Bhoushan, and France Bhattacharya. De La Forêt: Roman. Paris: Zulma, 2020.

Bertalanffy, Ludwig von. General System Theory: Foundations, Development, Applications. Rev. Ed. New-York: Braziller, 1968.

Bertin, Jacques, Serge Bonin, Jean-Daniel Gronoff, and Alexandra Laclau. La Graphique Et Le Traitement Graphique De L'information. Brussels: Zones sensibles, 2017.

Bonnefoy, Yves. Le Nuage Rouge: Essais Sur La Poétique. Paris: Mercure de France, 1992.

Bonnet, Emmanuel, Diego Landivar, and Alexandre Monnin. Héritage Et Fermeture: Une Écologie Du Démantèlement. Paris: Éditions Divergences, 2021.

Boutang, Moulier Yann, and Philippe Aigrain. Le Capitalisme Cognitif: La Nouvelle Grande Transformation. Paris: Éditions Amsterdam, 2008.

"Climate Change 2022: Impacts, Adaptation and Vulnerability." Intergovernmental Panel on Climate Change. Accessed 25 August 2022. www.ipcc.ch/report/ar6/wg2/.

Degros, Aglaée, Anna Bagarić, Sabine Bauer, Radostina Radulova-Stahmer, Mario Stefan, and Eva Schwab. Basics of Urbanism: 12 Begriffe der territorialen Transformation = 12 Notions of Territorial Transformation. Zurich: Park Books, 2021.

Deleuze, Gilles, and Félix Guattari. Mille Plateaux: Capitalisme Et Schizophrénie 2. Paris: Éditions de minuit, 1980.

"Démarche Du Parlement De Loire." POLAU, 1 July 2022. https://polau.org/incubations/demarche-du-parlement-de-loire/.

"Europan" Europan.eu, 2022. https:// www.europan-europe.eu/en/.

Fosse, Julien. "Objectif " Zéro Artificialisation Nette. Quels Leviers Pour Protéger Les Sols?" Accueil. Accessed December 15, 2022. https://www.strategie.gouv.fr/publications/objectif-zero-artificialisation-nette-leviers-proteger-sols.

Fussler, Urs. "Das Carambole-Prinzip", archplus, Zeitschrift für Architektur und Städtebau, 166, 2003.

"Geographic Information System." Wikipedia. Wikimedia Foundation, 14 December 2022. https://en.wikipedia. org/wiki/Geographic_information_ system.

Goutal, Jeanne Burgart. Être Écoféministe Théories Et Pratiques. 1st ed. Paris: Editions L'échappée, 2020.

Grulois, Geoffrey, Maria Chiara Tosi, and Carles Crosas. Designing Territorial Metabolism: Barcelona, Brussels, and Venice. Berlin: Jovis, 2018.

Güleş, Orhan, and Eva Schweitzer. "Künstliche Intelligenz Und Stadtentwicklung." Informationen zur Raumentwicklung. Franz Steiner Verlag, 1 September 2021. https://elibrary. steiner-verlag.de/article/99.105010/izr202103001201.

"Gwyneth Paltrow's Goop Encourages You to Pee in the Shower." Accessed 22 August 2022. https://www. cosmopolitan.com/health-fitness/news/a43799/gwyneth-paltrow-goop-pee-in-the-shower/.

Haff, Peter K. "Being Human in the Anthropocene." The Anthropocene Review 4, no. 2 (2017): 103–9. https://doirg/10.1177/2053019 617700875.

Hails, Chris. Rep. Living Planet Report 2006. Global Footprint Network, 2006. https://d2ouvy59podg6k. cloudfront. net/downloads/ living_planet_report. pdf.

Handke, Peter, Georges-Arthur Goldschmidt, Hermann Lenz, and Hanne Lenz. La Leçon De La Sainte-Victoire. Paris: Gallimard, 1991.

Holl, Christian, Felix Nowak, Kai Vöckler, and Peter Cachola Schmal. Living the Region. Tübingen: Ernst Wasmuth, 2018.

Ingold, Tim. The Life of Lines. London: Routledge Taylor & Francis Group, 2015.

Jackson, Tim. Prosperity without Growth: Foundations for the Economy of Tomorrow. London: Routledge, 2016.

KOSEC, Milos. 'An Architectural Jam-Session', unpublished manuscript intended for the also never published book 'Reusism' edited by Boštjan Vuga, Simon Hartmann, and Dijana Vučinić, 2016.

Latour, Bruno. Facing Gaia: Eight Lectures on the New Climate Regime/ Bruno Latour. Polity: United Kingdom, 2017.

Latour, Bruno. OÙ Suis-Je? Leçons Du Confinement à L'usage Des Terrestres. Paris: Éditions La Découverte, 2021.

Laumonier, Alexandre. 4. Paris: Zones sensibles, 2019.

Leclercq, François and Sabbah, Catherine. "Loger Mobile. Sans tourner en rond", Colloques de Cerisy. Loger mobiles, le logement au défi des mobilités. Le Centre culturel international de Cerisy. Cerisy-la-Salle, 11 June 2022.

Liu, Cixin, and Ken Liu. The Three-Body Problem. New York: Tor, 2016.

"Luma Days." LUMA Arles. Accessed 22 August 2022. https://www.luma.org/en/ arles/about-us/the-projects/luma-days. html.

Lynch, Kevin, and Michael Southworth. Wasting Away. San Francisco: Sierra Club Books, 1991.

Lynch, Kevin. L'image De La Cité. Paris: Dunod, 1969.

Lynch, Kevin. What Time Is This Place? Cambridge, Mass: MIT, 1972.

Macy, Joanna. "Agir avec le désespoir environnemental", in Hache, E. RECLAIM: Anthologie de textes écoféministes. Paris: Cambourakis, 2016.

Mangin, David, and Philippe Panerai. Projet Urbain. Marseille: Éd. Parenthèses, 2005.

Mantziaras, Panos. "Territorial Design in Geneva and Luxembourg – Lecture Panos Mantziaras." Vimeo, 2022. https://vimeo.com/698517207.

Mars, Roman, and Kurt Kohlstedt. The 99% Invisible City: A Field Guide to the Hidden World of Everyday Design. London: Hodder & Stoughton Ltd, 2020.

"Masterplan Radoffensive Graz 2030." Groove, 28 June 2022. https://groove. graz.at/.

Michaux, Henri. Saisir. Montpelier: Fata Morgana, 1979.

Mies, Maria, and Vandana Shiva. Ecofeminism. 2nd ed. London: Zed Books, 2014.

Munarin, Stefano, and Maria Chiara Tosi. Tracce Di Città: Esplorazioni Di Un Territorio Abitato: L'area Veneta. Milan: Angeli, 2002.

"Network." network Définition – Anglais Dictionnaire | network Explications et Prononciations. Accessed 15 December 2022. http://fr.dictionary.education./ english/dictionary/network.

Panerai, Philippe, Jean Castex, and Jean-Charles Depaule. Formes Urbaines: De L'îlot à La Barre. Marseille: Parenthèses, 1997.

Picon, Antoine. La Ville Territoire Des Cyborgs. Besançon: Les Éd. de l'Imprimeur, 1998.

Plan Urbanisme Construction Architecture. "Concours Amiter – Mieux Aménager Les Territoires En Mutation Exposés Aux Risques Naturels." Plan Urbanisme Construction Architecture, 10 May 2021. http://www.urbanisme-puca.gouv.fr/concours-amiter-mieux-amenager-les-territoires-en-a2213.html.

Pollo, Riccardo, and Matteo Trane. "Adaptation, Mitigation, and Smart Urban Metabolism towards the Ecological Transition." IRIS. Palermo University Press, 3 January 2022. iris. polito.it/handle/11583/2872597.

Recki, Birgit, and Frank Fehrenbach. Natur Und Technik: Eine Komplikation. 1st ed. Berlin: Matthes & Seitz, 2021.

Reed, Chris, and Nina-Marie E. Lister. Projective Ecologies. 2nd ed. Cambridge (MA): Harvard University Graduate school of design, 2020.

Remaud, Olivier, and Anne-Marie Garat. Penser Comme Un Iceberg. Arles: Actes Sud, 2020.

Rilke, Rainer Maria C'est le paysage longtemps. Verges collection. Paris: Edition Gallimard, 1978.

Shach-Pinsly, Dalit. "Digital Urban Regeneration and Its Impact on Urban Renewal Processes and Development: Editorial." Urban Planning, 17 November 2021. https:// www.cogitatiopress.com/ urbanplanning/article/ view/4905.

Shepard, Jim, and Hélène Papot. Le Maître Des Miniatures. Bruxelles: Vies Parallèles, 2017.

Sijmons. Landscape and Energy: Designing Transition. Rotterdam: naio10, 2014.

"Soil and People", Luxembourg in Transition, 2022. https:// luxembourgintransition.lu/wp-content/ uploads/2021/06/2phase_2001-komprimiert.pdf.

Spretnak, Charlene. Resurgence of the Real: Body, Nature and Place in a Hypermodern World. Taylor and Francis, 2012.

"Territoriaal Ontwikkelings- programma Noordrand", https://www.topnoordrand. be.

Thomas S. Kuhn. The Essential Tension: Tradition and Innovation in Scientific Research (Chicago: University of Chicago Press, 1959); The Structure of Scientific Revolutions (Chicago: University of Chicago Press, 1962)

Appendix

Ungers, O. M., Rem Koolhaas, Peter Riemann, Hans Kollhoff, Arthur Ovaska, Florian Hertweck, and Sébastien Marot. The City in the City: Berlin: A Green Archipelago. Zurich: Lars Müller Publishers, 2013.

Ursprung, Philip. Herzog & De Meuron: Natural History ; Accompanies the Exhibition "Herzog & De Meuron: Archaeology of the Mind", Organized by the Canadian Centre for Architecture (CCA), Montreal ; CCA from 23 October 2002 to 6 April 2003 ... Montreal: Canadian Centre for Architecture, 2002.

Viganò, Paola, Lorenzo Fabian, and Bernardo Secchi. Water and Asphalt: The Project of Isotropy. Zurich: Park Books, 2016.

Younès, Chris. "Europan Lecture", From productive cities to living cities. E15/E16 Virtual Inter-Sessions Forum – News. Europan. Accessed 11 August 2022. https://www.europan-europe.eu/en/news/e15-e16-virtual-inter-sessions-forum.

Zalasiewicz, Jan, Colin N. Waters, Colin P. Summerhayes, Alexander P. Wolfe, Anthony D. Barnosky, Alejandro Cearreta, Paul Crutzen, et al. "The Working Group on the Anthropocene: Summary of Evidence and Interim Recommendations." Anthropocene. Elsevier, 8 September 2017. https://www.science-direct.com/science/article/pii/S2213305417300097

Image credits

Fig. 01–21: AWP

Fig. 22/23: ALS_O (Artgineering, LAMA, SWECO, Daniel Ost)

Fig. 24-28: Artgineering

Fig. 29: Institute of Urbanism, Graz University of Technology

Fig. 30-33: Sandra Freudenthaler

Fig. 34: Mendi Kocis, Mara Lang, Carina Mazelle, Katrin Neumann, Master Studio Rewilding Bad Gastein, Aglaée Degros, Klaus K. Loenhart, Anna Bagaric, Patricia Lucena Ventura, SS 2021, Institute of Urbanism, Institute of Architecture and Landscape, Graz University of Technology

Fig. 35: Gallinca

Fig. 36–74: AWP et al.

P. 62-87: Anna Positano

Fig. 75: GSD Harvard

Fig. 76: IRS Institut de recherches sociologiques UniGe

Fig. 77: Gaëla Blandy

Fig. 78: Graz University of Technology

Fig. 79: Radostina Radulova-Strahmer

Fig. 80: AWP

Fig. 81: Brouez Aymerick, International Master in Ecological Urbanism, Matthias Armengaud, Ingrid Taillandier, École nationale supérieure d'architecture de Versailles 2021

Fig. 82–88: Brouez Aymerick, International Master in Ecological Urbanism, Matthias Armengaud, Ingrid Taillandier, École nationale supérieure d'architecture de Versailles 2021

Fig. 89-90: Mendi Kocis, Master Studio Luxemburg in Transition, Aglaée Degros, Radostina Radulova-Stahmer, SS 2021, Institute of Urbanism, Graz University of Technology

P. 144–145: Anna Positano

Fig. 91: AWP

Fig. 92-94: Brouez Aymerick, International Master in Ecological Urbanism, Matthias Armengaud, Ingrid Taillandier, École nationale supérieure d'architecture de Versailles 2021

Fig. 95-101: Caitlin Lam Tze Ting and Beazi Alizée, International Master in Ecological Urbanism, Matthias Armengaud, Ingrid Taillandier, École nationale supérieure d'architecture de Versailles 2021

Fig. 102-108: Soohye Jeong and Cécile Kermaïdic, International Master in Ecological Urbanism, Matthias Armengaud, Ingrid Taillandier, École nationale supérieure d'architecture de Versailles 2021

Fig. 109-112: Carina Mazelle, Master Studio Luxemburg in Transition, Aglaée Degros, Radostina Radulova-Stahmer, SS 2021, Institute of Urbanism, Graz University of Technology

P. 156–157: Anna Positano

Fig. 113: AWP

Fig. 114: Le Cornec Roman, International Master in Ecological Urbanism, Matthias Armengaud, Ingrid Taillandier, École nationale supérieure d'architecture de Versailles 2021

Fig. 115-123: Le Cornec Roman, International Master in Ecological Urbanism, Matthias Armengaud, Ingrid Taillandier, École nationale supérieure d'architecture de Versailles 2021

Fig. 124-131: Salila Sihou and Pino Heye, International Master in Ecological Urbanism, Matthias Armengaud, Ingrid Taillandier, École nationale supérieure d'architecture de Versailles 2021

Fig. 132-137: Micaela Sepulveda, International Master in Ecological Urbanism, Matthias Armengaud, Ingrid Taillandier, École nationale supérieure d'architecture de Versailles 2021

Fig. 138-141: Carola Hilgert, Master Studio Luxemburg in Transition, Aglaée Degros, Radostina Radulova-Stahmer, SS 2021, Institute of Urbanism, Graz University of Technology

P. 168-169: Anna Positano

Fig. 142: AWP

Fig. 143: Peziere Loris, International Master in Ecological Urbanism, Matthias Armengaud, Ingrid Taillandier, École nationale supérieure d'architecture de Versailles 2021

Fig. 144-149: Marie-Theres Schwaighofer, Master Studio Luxemburg in Transition, Aglaée Degros, Radostina Radulova-Stahmer, SS 2021, Institute of Urbanism, Graz University of Technology

Fig. 150-154: Marie-Theres Schwaighofer, Master Studio Luxemburg in Transition, Aglaée Degros, Radostina Radulova-Stahmer, SS 2021, Institute of Urbanism, Graz University of Technology

P. 178-179: Anna Positano

Fig. 155: AWP

Fig. 156-163: Ciceri Louise, International Master in Ecological Urbanism, Matthias Armengaud, Ingrid Taillandier, École nationale supérieure d'architecture de Versailles 2021

Appendix

Fig. 164-169: Gaelle Dechenaux and Suzanne Brigaud, International Master in Ecological Urbanism, Matthias Armengaud, Ingrid Taillandier, École nationale supérieure d'architecture de Versailles 2021

Fig. 170-173: Rhita Adnane and Maria Zboralska, International Master in Ecological Urbanism, Matthias Armengaud, Ingrid Taillandier, École nationale supérieure d'architecture de Versailles 2021

Fig. 174-176: Beatrice Wagner, Master Studio Luxemburg in Transition, Aglaée Degros, Radostina Radulova-Stahmer, SS 2021, Institute of Urbanism, Graz University of Technology

P. 188–189: Anna Positano

Fig. 177: AWP

Fig. 178/179: Myriam Oba, International Master in Ecological Urbanism, Matthias Armengaud, Ingrid Taillandier, École nationale supérieure d'architecture de Versailles 2021

Fig. 180-184: Myriam Oba, International Master in Ecological Urbanism, Matthias Armengaud, Ingrid Taillandier, École nationale supérieure d'architecture de Versailles 2021

Fig. 185/186: Philipp Misterek, Master Studio Luxemburg in Transition, Aglaée Degros, Radostina Radulova-Stahmer, SS 2021, Institute of Urbanism, Graz University of Technology

P. 196–197: Anna Positano

Fig. 187: based on 51N4E et al. adapted by AWP

Fig. 188: based on yellow z et al. adapted by the Institute of Urbanism, Graz University of Technology

Fig. 189: based on Centre de recherche Habitat et al. adapted by AWP

Fig. 190: based on Artgineering et al. adapted by the Institute of Urbanism, Graz University of Technology

Fig. 191: based on brechtholdkrass space&options et al. adapted by the Institute of Urbanism, Graz University of Technology

Fig. 192: based on AWP et al. adapted by AWP

Colophon

Editors
Matthias Armengaud, Aglaée Degros with Radostina Radulova-Stahmer

Editing
Paride Zambelli and Bérénice Gentil with Enora Cloitre, Akhilesh Shisodia, Carina Mazzelle, Carina Fechter, Lukas Schneider, Johannes Bernsteiner

Editoral manager
Eva Guttman

Copy editing and proofreading
Susannah Leopold

Proofreading
Y'plus Graz

Design
AWP Agence de reconfiguration territoriale

Graphics
AWP Agence de reconfiguration territoriale, Institute of Urbanism Graz University of Technology

Layout support and lithography
Atelier Neubacher Graz

Printing and binding
Medienfabrik Graz GmbH

Copyright for the texts: the authors
Copyright for all photographs:
Anna Positano

Park Books
Niederdorfstrasse 54
8001 Zurich
Switzerland
www.park-books.com

Park Books is being supported by the Federal Office of Culture with a general subsidy for the years 2021–2024.

All rights reserved; no part of this publication may be reproduced, stored in a retrieval system or transmitted in any form or by any means, electronic, mechanical, photocopying, recording, or otherwise, without the prior written consent of the publisher.

ISBN 978-3-03860-305-4

© 2023 AWP, Institute of Urbanism, Graz University of Technology, and Park Books AG, Zurich

This book was published with the support of:
École nationale supérieure d'architecture de Versailles (https://www.versailles.archi.fr/fr)
Graz University of Technology (https://www.tugraz.at/home/)

École nationale supérieure d'architecture Versailles